STICKLEY BROTHERS

FURNITURE

IDENTIFICATION & VALUE GUIDE

Larry Koon

COLLECTOR BOOKS

A Division of Schroeder Publishing Co., Inc.

Front cover, clockwise from top right: Gustav Stickley armchair, $1,100.00; Gustav Stickley shelf clock, $9,200.00; Gustav Stickley china cabinet, $9,000.00; Gustav Stickley tall-back chair, $1,200.00 – 1,800.00; L. & J. G. Stickley sideboard, $6,500.00; Gustav Stickley tabouret, $2,400.00; Stickley Brothers settle, $10,000.

Cover design by Beth Summers
Book design by Heather Warren

COLLECTOR BOOKS
P.O. Box 3009
Paducah, Kentucky 42002-3009

www.collectorbooks.com

Copyright © 2004 Larry Koon

The current values in this book should be used only as a guide. They are not intended to set prices, which vary from one section of the country to another. Auction prices as well as dealer prices vary greatly and are affected by condition as well as demand. Neither the author nor the publisher assumes responsibility for any losses that might be incurred as a result of consulting this guide.

Searching For A Publisher?

We are always looking for people knowledgeable within their fields. If you feel that there is a real need for a book on your collectible subject and have a large comprehensive collection, contact Collector Books.

All photographs throughout this price guide are courtesy of David Rago Auctions unless noted as Craftman Auction photos.

Contents

Dedication

I would like to dedicate this book to its main character, Gustav Stickley, who most inspired me to write it. A man whose dreams and career were cut short by a large group of competitors, including his four younger brothers, brothers who later went on to gain fame and fortune by copying their oldest brother's work, his original plans, his dreams, and his life.

"To my most wonderful customers: Most of my furniture was so carefully designed and well proportioned in the first place that even I, with my advanced experience, cannot improve upon it."

Gustav Stickley

Acknowledgments

First of all, I would like to thank David Rago Auctions (www.ragoarts.com) in Lambertville, New Jersey, for giving me rights to use many of its auction photos throughout this guide, and sending me many prices realized from the sale of Stickley Brothers furniture. I especially want to thank Anthony Barnes with David Rago Auctions for preparing the digital photos I needed for this guide. Also, I want to thank Suzanne with Craftsman Auctions in Pittsfield, Massachusetts for also supplying photos for this guide, and I would like to thank Craftsman Farms and the Gustav Stickley Museum in Parsippany-Troy Hills, New Jersey, for filling me in on the life of Gustav Stickley. I would like to express my appreciation to the L. & J. G. Stickley Furniture Company in Manlius, New York, as well, for providing information about the Stickley brothers.

I especially want to thank the greatest mom in the world, who passed away on June 14, 1998, for putting up with me all those years, since I was 12 years old and trying to write my first million seller (ha ha). I also want to thank my publisher, Schroeder Publishing Company, for giving me a contract for this book. To everyone I may have neglected to mention who supplied me with information about the Stickley brothers, I just want to say that you're all the greatest people in the world.

Yours sincerely,
Larry Koon

4

About the Author

Larry Koon, author of the *Stickley Brothers Furniture Identification and Value Guide*, is also the author of *Roycroft Furniture and Collectibles* for Collector Books and author of *Annalee Dolls Price Guide* for Portfolio Press. He also writes a weekly column for the *Marrietta Times*, Marietta, Ohio. Larry's goal is to write more price guides, especially resource guides for today's collectors.

Larry hails from Ripley, West Virginia, and resides in Belpre, Ohio.

Introduction

Welcome to the first edition of the *Stickley Brothers Furniture Identification and Value Guide*, laid out in four complete chapters about five very famous brothers: Gustav, Charles, Albert, John, and Leopold Stickley, makers of fine furniture and accessories, who were each separately involved at different times and at different workshops in designing and producing their own furniture lines such as bookcases, dressers, chests of drawers, sideboards, beds, and other furniture items during the Arts and Crafts movement. Each one's work was entirely based on oldest brother Gustav Stickley's original ideas and plans concerning the making of furniture. Throughout each chapter of this comprehensive price guide, you'll find every make and model of furniture the brothers ever crafted that had been sold in the last few years on the auction block. A collection of furniture this comprehensive has never before been published and made available to furniture dealers and collectors around the country.

Chapter I deals with the furniture of Gustav Stickley, the oldest of the five brothers and the one whose work is most highly regarded. In 1898, at his workshop in Eastwood, New York, he developed a line of mission furniture that has a European style. Just recently, a bookcase Gustav Stickley crafted sometime between 1901 and 1903 sold at auction for $77,500. Another bookcase, model 700½, was recently sold at auction for $22,000, and a chest of drawers made by Gustav Stickley in 1902 went for $32,000 at auction. Much of Gustav Stickley's earlier furniture can be found with a red decal. Sometimes it was signed, and sometimes it bore a joiner's compass and the words "Als Ik Kan"; it was produced in a variety of models and sizes.

Gustav Stickley produced furniture from 1898 until 1915, when competition and a loss of public interest in Mission-style furniture forced him to go out of business and declare bankruptcy. Stickley's competitors included his four younger brothers, who later gained fame and fortune by copying their older brother's work and selling their pieces at much lower prices. Gustav Stickley died in 1941, at the age of 84.

Chapter II focuses on the furniture made by the Stickley Brothers Furniture Company, a firm founded in 1892 by Charles and Albert Stickley, two of Gustav Stickley's younger brothers. The firm was located in Binghampton, New York, and Grand Rapids, Michigan. Albert and John Stickley ran the company in Michigan, and Charles ran the company in Binghampton; he and an uncle operated the business for several years as the Stickley/Brandt Furniture Company. After several years with the company in Michigan, John left to join his brother Leopold in Fayetteville, New York, where together they formed their own company, called L. & J. G. Furniture, still in business today in Manlius, New York. Much of their original furniture in the Colonial Williamsburg style is reproduced today. See Chapter III of this guide for information about L. & J. G. furniture; Charles Stickley also produced a line of his own furniture, and that is covered in Chapter IV.

The Stickley Brothers Furniture Company first started out producing furniture with very fine inlay, decorations, and cutouts. Its furniture can be found today with a paper label that reads, "Made by Stickley Brothers, Grand Rapids, Michigan," or sometimes found with a brass plate or decal with the words "Quaint Furniture." The company produced metal accessories and copper items, as well as a very popular furniture line that included desks, bookcases, armchairs, china cabinets, rockers, sideboards, and other furniture and accessories for the home. The company operated from 1901 to 1954.

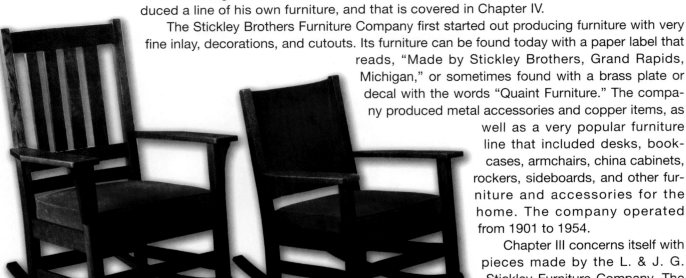

Chapter III concerns itself with pieces made by the L. & J. G. Stickley Furniture Company. The company was founded in 1900, by Gustav Stickley's two younger brothers Leopold and John Stickley. Over the years, the company produced a variety of items that are most sought after today, such as armchairs, bookcases, desks, and other furniture, many of which are photographed and priced throughout Chapter III of this guide.

The company first operated under the name of Onondaga Shops, and was originally located in Fayetteville, New York. Its furniture was very well constructed and was well marketed, and can still be found all around the country today. The business eventually became very successful. All items the company produced contained a decal that said either "Handcraft" or "Onondaga Shops" and had each brother's initials; *L. & J. G.* stands for Leopold and John George Stickley. The company is still in business today and is located in Manlius, New York. Much of its furniture continues to be produced in the Colonial Williamsburg style.

Chapter IV takes a look at the furniture produced by Charles Stickley, who originally ran the Stickley Furniture Company in Binghampton, New York, along with his uncle, under the name Stickley/Brandt Furniture. Much of this furniture found today has either the Charles Stickley signature or a Stickley/Brandt decal. These decals were made in several different sizes. The furniture does not command the price today that other Stickley furniture does, but it is still most sought after by furniture dealers and collectors all over the country.

Enough said about the famous Stickley brothers. Sit back and enjoy the most comprehensive price guide ever published about Stickley Brothers furniture.

Gustav Stickley's American Mission

Gustav Stickley is thought by some to be the most talented craftsman to ever play an important role in the Arts and Crafts movement. He was born in Osceola, Wisconsin, in 1858. The son of an immigrant, he learned to make furniture at a very young age, at a chair factory owned by an uncle. Years later, after taking over the factory, he moved it to New York state, first to Binghampton and then to Syracuse.

Being influenced by the Arts and Crafts movement and by visits to old missions in the American Southwest, in 1900 Gustav Stickley introduced a highly original line of sturdy oak furniture that he made in his workshop in Eastwood, New York; it consisted of mission furniture, which contains little or no decoration at all, with a style that was noticeably European.

The furniture was first introduced to a wide audience in the summer of 1900 by the Tobey Furniture Company of Chicago, Illinois, after a buyer for the company had seen Stickley's furniture on display at a Grand Rapids, Michigan, furniture exposition and purchased the entire lot. The company began to sell Stickley's new furniture line, which included over 75 different chairs, tables, stools, and desks. Gustav Stickley soon severed his ties with the company and began marketing his furniture on his own.

In 1901, he adopted the name of his new furniture company, calling it United Crafts, and began publishing his own furniture catalog, the *Craftsman*. This catalog enabled him to promote his furniture throughout the country. The catalog also taught do-it-yourselfers how to build their own Mission-style furniture. The *Craftsman* was also distributed to many schools around the country as a way of supporting vocational training in the making of chests, trestles, gateleg tables, and settles.

In 1904, Gustav Stickley renamed his company Craftsman Workshops, and profit sharing was terminated as the company began to expand. Over 200 workers were hired; the company then began to evolve through several different phases. Initially, furniture lacked the quality of Gustav Stickley's earlier pieces. Stickley rarely used the tenon and key joints as found in earlier furniture and began to select very thin wood in the making of his furniture. Not securing his dowels as on earlier pieces, Stickley also eliminated all Art Nouveau detailing on his furniture.

Furniture later became much heavier, which revealed Stickley's earlier training as a stonemason. Believing in excellent quality, Gustav Stickley began using protruding tenons, fastened with keys, that exposed dovetails and butterfly joints. Splines in dadoes, or E-joints, were also used to hold backboards together. Stickley also began using American white oak in the making of furniture that was quartersawn, in order to eliminate cracking and warping. Every piece of furniture was also stained to a rich brown color by the process of fuming with ammonia. Library tables were often made covered with leather, and for durable surfaces on tables to be used as plant stands, Stickley used tiles that were originally purchased from the famous Grueby Pottery in Boston. Stickley also began developing new hardware for each piece of furniture, not using the brass pulls that are found on his earlier furniture. Oval and round pulls that Stickley later used on furniture were hand wrought and were made of copper, brass, or iron that contained V-shaped bales attached with large faceted nails to the wood.

The years 1904 to 1910 were the most profitable years for Gustav Stickley and his Craftsman workshops. He began following an industry wide trend by using wide laminated oak panels, and started replacing chamfered boards on the backs of all bookcases and desks with V-joints. Tenon and key construction was seldom used, because veneer became more common and cheaper to use. In 1910, Stickley also stopped making spindle furniture and entirely eliminated the Harvey Ellis–inspired curves on the furniture he made. In Gustav Stickley's final years of production, his furniture also became more rectilinear and stripped of structural details. After 1910, a brand name replaced the red decal on all his furniture, which had portrayed a joiner's compass and had had the words "Als-Ik-Kan." Some pieces of furniture showing up at auctions around the country today have been found with Craftsman paper labels or with Eastwood paper labels. Black labels have also been found on some furniture. Some of the furniture also included a model number; each model was produced in many different sizes.

One of the most popular pieces of furniture Gustav Stickley ever produced was a better-quality version, which he patented in 1901, of the famous Morris chair. It had a reclining back, but had square spindles supporting the arms that were able to be adjusted by fitting a rod into holes or notches; the original Morris chairs used wide slats. Stickley's chair is known today as a reclining chair, sometimes called a reading chair. It is similar to other spindle furniture pieces Gustav Stickley made in 1904 that are shown throughout this guide. These earlier chairs had cushions that were supported by caned or rope seats. In 1906, canvas seats were first introduced, and in 1909, springs were added to the seat. Leather and linen were also used to cover cushions. Occasionally, chairs with rush used to support the seats are found today.

Many claimed that Gustav Stickley's earlier furniture was much too monotonous, so he began offering a new line of willow furniture, particularly sofas, which were called "settles," and armchairs. These most popular pieces of furniture were usually painted a soft green or a deep brown color, and had canvas-covered cushions. Stickley promoted this furniture line in catalogs alongside his dark oak furniture that could be used in summer cottages and was well-suited for use on sun porches.

Other craftsmen used rattan vine that was imported from Germany or the Far East to make willow furniture; it was less expensive to use than willow. They wove the rattan leaf into seats and backs, and used the reed stem for the chair frames. Chairs were then shellacked, or painted white, black, or green. These chairs have shown up at auctions over the years also painted red or other colors.

Gustav Stickley's American Mission Comes to a Close

Although Gustav Stickley was not the first craftsman to introduce Mission-style furniture, he came closer than anyone to dominating the field. He used his own original European design and never once tried to capitalize on Joseph McHughes's earlier California Spanish style.

In 1915, Gustav Stickley's career was cut short when he was forced out of business by a large group of competitors. This group included his four younger brothers, who were copying his work and selling their versions at much lower prices. This competition, combined with a loss of public interest in Mission-style furniture, led to Stickley's declaration of bankruptcy. It has been theorized that Gustav Stickley had very much overextended his large empire by purchasing the 12-story Craftsman building in New York City just as the public's preference of furniture shifted to Colonial Revival. Although Gustav Stickley later came out with his own Revival-style furniture, Chromewald, it was too late.

After declaring bankruptcy, Gustav Stickley went to work for his two brothers John and Leopold, owners of L. & J. G. Stickley Furniture; they had bought his factory. This relationship between Gustav Stickley and these two brothers did not last long. Gustav Stickley's brothers, Albert, Charles, John, and Leopold, went on to gain fame and fortune from their oldest brother's original ideas and furniture designs.

Gustav Stickley died in 1942, at the age of 84. His work and his talent continue to live on today, well displayed in many Victorian homes around the country. His furniture was indeed "so carefully designed and proportioned in the first place" that no one, not even Gustav Stickley, could have ever improved upon it.

Gustav Stickley Museum

The log home that Gustav Stickley and his family once lived in (from 1908 to 1917) in Parsippany, New Jersey, is today a national historic landmark owned by the Township of Parsippany and is operated by the Craftsman Museum Farms Foundation, a non-profit organization focusing on educating the public about the ideas and beliefs of Gustav Stickley.

Stickley, who originally hailed from Wisconsin, was the son of a German immigrant chair maker. He began his Craftsman era with the purchase of this property in 1908. In 1917, just two years after declaring bankruptcy, Gustav Stickley sold the property to a family named Farny. In 1989, when the Farny family was about to sell the property to a real estate developer, the Parsippany Township stepped in and purchased the property, and its care and management were turned over to the non-profit foundation called Craftsman Farms Foundation. Today, the foundation is continuing to restore the property to its original appearance. According to Craftsman Farms, the main building on the property is a sort of clubhouse. The offices of the foundation, as well as the living quarters, are housed in the main building, which today is preserved and decorated the same way as when Gustav Stickley and his family left it in 1917. A gift shop is also housed in the main building; here, reproductions of Arts and Crafts–era pieces are sold, along with a large assortment of books relating to the Arts and Crafts era. The grounds of Gustav Stickley's former home are open to visitors every day.

The Stickley Museum is open April through November, from noon until 3:00 p.m. Wednesday through Friday and from 11:00 a.m. until 4:00 p.m. on Saturday.

For information about requesting a tour of Gustav Stickley's former home, telephone Craftsman Farms at (973) 540-1165.

Directions to the Gustav Stickley museum:

The entrance of Craftsman Farms is located on Route 10 West at Powder Mills Estates, about 3 miles west of I-287 in Parsippany-Troy Hills, New Jersey.

You can also visit the museum's website at www.stickleymuseum.org, or shop online at the Stickley Museum Gift Shop at http://stickleymuseumshop.safeshopper.com/.

The museum publishes a newsletter entitled *Notes from the Farms.* It is published periodically throughout the year.

Gustav Stickley Museum mailing address:
Gustav Stickley Museum
c/o Craftsman Farms Foundation
2352 Route 10 West, Box 5
Morris Plains, NJ 07950
Craftsman Farms Foundation telephone number: 973-540-1165
Craftsman Farms Foundation e-mail address: setabit@njskylands.com
Craftsman Farms foundation website: http://njskylands.com/hscrfarm.htm

Buying and Selling Resources

Auction Service

David Rago Auctions of Lambertville, New Jersey, is the leading American auction house specializing in the buying and selling of Stickley Brothers furniture. No other auction house in the country is more knowledgeable or better qualified to handle transactions between buyers and sellers in this thriving market of twentieth-century arts and furnishings. No other auction company offers a stronger warranty. The auction company also takes particular pride in providing expertise without attitude and without many of the small incremental charges levied by others in their field. Today, David Rago is in partnership with Jerry Cohen and John Fontaine as Craftsman Auctions, holding three weekend Arts and Crafts auctions in its New Jersey facility. One thousand lots of the best in Mission arts and furnishings are offered every September, January, and May.

To consign Stickley brothers furniture or to sell outright, contact David Rago Auctions, 333 North Main Street, Lambertville, NJ 08530. Telephone: (609) 397-9374. Fax: (609) 397-9377. Internet address: www.ragoarts.com. To order its latest catalogs, telephone 1-866-724-6278.

Abbreviation Guide

AI — As Is

AVG — Average

AVG+ — Above Average

FR — Fair

G — Good

VG — Very Good

EX — Excellent

F — Fine

M — Mint

Gustav Stickley Furniture
(1898 – 1915)

Much of Gustav Stickley's furniture was marked with several different brands and labels. His early furniture, made in conjunction with the Tobey Furniture Company of Chicago, does not bear his name. However, in 1901 he introduced his well-known brand and decal that featured a joiner's compass and the words "Als Ik Kan," which stand for "as well as I can." Over the next fourteen years, the mark was periodically altered. In 1901, it took the form of a brand, with the initials "GS" within the compass and "Als Ik Kan" in a rectangular box, followed by "Gustav Stickley, Cabinet Maker, Syracuse, New York."

During the years 1902 – 1904, the mark was a similar red decal, and it was entirely enclosed within a bordering rectangle.

From 1904 to 1912, furniture lacked the bordering rectangle, and for the first time, the signature "Gustav Stickley" was used rather than just "Stickley." Sometimes, a red decal was used. Some pieces made between 1910 and 1912 were stamped in black.

From 1912 through 1915, Stickley's mark was a black brand consisting of the joiner's compass and "Stickley."

From 1905 through 1907, Gustav Stickley used several printed paper labels in conjunction with decals or brands. These read: "Trademark / The Craftsman Workshops / Gustav Stickley / Designed and Made By / Gustav Stickley / Eastwood, New York, illustrating the compass and Als Ik Kan reading the name 'Craftsman' is our / registered trademark and / identifies all our furniture / Craftsman / Made by Gustav Stickley in the / Craftsman Workshops / Eastwood, New York / New York City Showrooms / at 29 West Thirty Fourth Street."

From 1912 through 1915, Gustav Stickley furniture carried a very lengthy label that read: "Craftsman / Trade / Marks / REG'D / in U.S. / Patent / Office / Stickley / This Paster together with my Device and Signature (Branded) on a / piece of furniture stands as my / Guarantee to the purchaser that / the piece is made with the same / care and earnestness that has / Characterized all my efforts / from the beginning and is meant that I would hold myself RE-Sponsible for any Defects in Mate- / rial workmanship or finish that / may be discovered by the pur- / chaser even after the piece has / been in use for a reasonable / length of time, and that I will either make good any defects or / take back the piece and refund / the purchase price / This piece was made in my / cabinet shops at Eastwood, New York / Signed Gustav Stickley."

Gustav Stickley blanket chest with paneled top and sides, joined by wrought iron strap hardware. Signed with 1902/1903 red decal. Original finish, excellent condition, 18" x 34¾" x 19¾". $27,500.00.

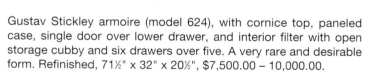

Gustav Stickley single bed, with arched top rail and three broad vertical slats both to the headboard and the footboard, broad side rails, and red decal. Refinished. Headboard 44" x 39". $1,200.00.

Gustav Stickley armoire (model 624), with cornice top, paneled case, single door over lower drawer, and interior filter with open storage cubby and six drawers over five. A very rare and desirable form. Refinished, 71½" x 32" x 20½", $7,500.00 – 10,000.00.

Gustav Sitckley Wardrobe, with two paneled doors. Interior contains five half drawers and one full drawer. Original finish with overcoat, paper label and decal. Good condition, 62" x 43" x 24". $8,000.00 – 10,000.00.
Photo courtesy of Craftsman Auctions.

Gustav Stickley cedar-lined chest, with strap hardware. Signed, excellent condition, 15" x 24" x 12". $46,000.00. *Photo courtesy of Craftsman Auctions.*

Gustav Stickley rare blanket box, with hinged and paneled top, panels to front and back, and spindled sides. Refinished, Eastwood paper label, excellent condition, 16" x 30" x 16". $4,750.00.

Gustav Stickley twin-size spindle bed, on casters, with new finish and branded mark. Excellent condition, 50½" x 79½" 45½". $1,900.00.

Set of two Gustav Stickley slatted single beds, headboards and footboards only. Fair condition, 43¾" x 39½". $450.00.

Gustav Stickley rare blanket box, with iron hardware and dovetailed sides. Excellent finish and condition, brand and paper label, 17¼" x 36" x 22". $4,000.00. *Photo courtesy of Craftsman Auctions.*

Not Shown

191 Bed, 5 vertical slats at side, 30" x 29", VG, early mark, $2,900.00.

216 Bed, 5 vertical slats at side, 80" x 31" x 29", VG, $4,025.00.

917 Bed, 3 wide slats, attached slats to posts, 58" x 54" x 80", EX, red decal, signed, $9,500.00.

919 Bed (child's), spindled, slots in headboard, 36" x 56" x 44", EX, red decal, $3,500.00 – 4,500.00.

922 Bed (full size), horizontal board, rounded posts, 59" x 78" x 58", EX, branded signature, $4,250.00.

922 Bed (full size), horizontal slats over horizontal board, 62" x 79" x 53", EX, Red decal, $6,000.00.

923 Bed (single), arched top rail, 75" x 41", EX, branded signature, $800.00.

923 Bed (full size), 5 wide slats, tapered legs, 59" x 78" x 48", VG, red decal, branded signature, $4,000.00.

923 Bed, original finish, minor restoration, 77" x 57" x 48", VG, $4,500.00.

Bed, maple, inlaid, pewter, Arts and Crafts design, 46" x 79" x 40", VG, signed, paper label, $2,100.00.

Bed (double), wooden rails, original finish, 37" x 49" x 58", EX, burned mark, $4,000.00.

Bed, vertical slats in headboard & footboard, 48" x 59" x 78", VG, signed, $8,000.00.

Bed, paneled headboard & footboard, 50" x 58", EX, $9,000.00.

Bed, vertical spindles, 50½" x 57½", VG, $1,600.00.

Bed (double), horizontal rail at back, 58" x 79" x 49", VG, red decal, signed, $3,500.00.

Bed (day bed), 5 slats at each end, 78" x 30" x 30", VG, $28,000.00.

Chest (blanket), paneled top and sides, 78" x 34¾" x 19¾", EX, red decal, signed, $27,500.00.

920 Wardrobe, 2-shelf interior, original finish, 45" x 16" x 70", EX, decal, $3,500.00.

920 Wardrobe (child's), iron V-pulls on panelled doors, 33" x 16½" x 60", VG, paper label, $4,675.00.

Wardrobe; iron V-pulls, hooks, clothing poles; 36" x 16" x 70", VG, brown decal, $3,500.00.

Wardrobe, 2-shelf interior, original finish, 45" x 16" x 70", EX, decal, $3,500.00.

Wardrobe, 2 paneled doors, copper pulls, 60" x 33" x 16", EX, signed, $23,000.00.

Gustav Stickley early 5-drawer chest, with arched backsplash, paneled sides and back, pyramid wooden pulls, original finish, and large red decal. Very good condition, 43" x 36" x 20". $8,000.00.

Gustav Stickley rare chest of drawers, with V-shaped backsplash, two short drawers over four long ones, hammered-copper pulls, and chamfered sides. Mint original condition, blackened paper label and red decal, 52½" x 52½" x 21¾". $32,000.00.

Early Gustav Stickley 6-drawer chest, with oval hammered-copper pulls, paneled sides, and light overcoat to original finish. Excellent condition, 50" x 41" x 22½". $6,000.00 – 7,000.00.

Gustav Stickley chest of drawers, with two drawers over four, scratches and chips, added drawer locks, and original finish. Signed, fair condition, 53" x 40" x 20½". $4,000.00 – 4,500.00.

Gustav Stickley 5-drawer chest (model 621), with iron pulls, panaled sides, two replaced boards, black ink mark, and original finish. Fair condition, 42" x 36" x 20½". $4,000.00 – 4,500.00.

Gustav Stickley chest of drawers, with five drawers, backsplash, hammered-copper pulls, paneled sides, original finish, and branded mark. Excellent condition, 42" x 36" x 20". $5,000.00.

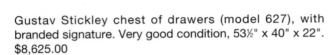

Gustav Stickley chest of drawers (model 627), with branded signature. Very good condition, 53½" x 40" x 22". $8,625.00

Early Gustav Stickley chest, with paneled back, two-drawers-over-four configuration, and oval copper drop pulls. Stripped finish, very good condition, 49½" x 40¾" x 22¼". $5,500.00.

Gustav Stickley rare 6-drawer chest, with arched back-splash, paneled sides, oval iron pulls (rare size), and cleaned original finish. Decal and paper label, very good condition, 53" x 29" x 20". $6,000.00.

626 Chest of drawers, 2 drawers over 4, iron pulls, 36" x 20" x 43", EX, dated 1904, black decal, $8,500.00.

626 Chest of Drawers, 2 drawers over 3, oval iron pulls, 36" x 20" x 43", EX, Eastwood label, signed, $8,500.00.

627 Chest of Drawers, 2 half drawers over 4 full, copper hardware, 40" x 23" x 53", VG, red decal, signed, $7,000.00.

902 Chest of Drawers, 2 drawers over 4 oval brass pulls, 42" x 23" x 54", EX, red decal, $16,000.00.

906 Chest of Drawers, 2 drawers over 4, iron pulls, paneled sides, 40" x 21" x 45", EX, red decal, signed, $8,250.00.

906 Chest of Drawers, 4 long drawers, copper pulls, 48" x 41" x 21", VG, red decal, signed, $8,500.00.

906 Chest of Drawers, 2 drawers over 4, iron pulls, 70" x 40" x 21", EX, paper label, branded signature, $20,000.00.

909 Chest of Drawers, 2 half drawers over 3 full, wooden knobs, 37" x 19" x 42", VG, red decal, signed, $2,600.00.

909 Chest of Drawers, 2 short drawers over 3 long, 42" x 36" x 20", VG, $2,700.00.

913 Chest of Drawers, 6 half drawers over 3 full, 37" x 36" x 20", VG, $1,200.00.

913 Chest of Drawers, 4 drawers, wooden pulls, 50" x 36" x 20", VG, red decal, $3,500.00.

90 Chest of Drawers, 2 half drawers over 4 full, 34" x 20" x 53", VG, "Handcraft" decal, $1,500.00.

Gustav Stickley rare dresser (model 915), curly maple, with original finish and red decal. Excellent condition, 42½" x 42" x 20". $16,000.00 – 18,000.00. *Photo courtesy of Craftsman Auctions.*

Early Gustav Stickley 5-drawer vanity, with hammered-copper drop pulls and pivoting mirror, flanked by copper candle sconces (one missing). Original finish, 1902 decal, excellent condition, 57" x 54" x 22". $9,000.00 – 10,000.00.

Gustav Stickley 4-drawer dresser (model 911), designed by Harvey Ellis, with pivoting mirror, hammered-copper V-pulls, and arched toe board. Original finish, branded mark, very good condition, 33" x 48" x 22". Mirror size, 33½" x 43". $9,000.00 – 10,000.00.

Gustav Stickley dresser (model 909), with backsplash, paneled sides, two-drawers-over-three configuration, and circular wooden pulls. Original finish, branded mark, very good condition, 42" x 36" x 20½". $3,500.00 – $4,000.00.

Gustav Stickley dresser, designed by Harvey Ellis, with tapering posts, two small drawers over two full, circular wooden pulls, arched apron, pivoting mirror, and new finish. Good condition, 32½" x 48" x 22". $1,600.00.

Gustav Stickley dresser, with backsplash, paneled sides, two-drawers-over-three configuration, and circular wooden pulls. Original finish, paper label, very good condition, 42" x 37" x 19½". $3,250.00.

Gustav Stickley dresser (model 911), designed by Harvey Ellis, with four drawers, arched toe board, circular wooden pulls, and mirror. Original finish and mirror, missing harp. Craftsman paper label, good condition, 61½" x 48" x 22". $2,750.00.

Gustav Stickley 4-drawer dresser (model 911), designed by Harvey Ellis, with pivoting mirror, hammered-copper V-pulls, and arched toe board. Original finish, red decal, very good condition, 48" x 22" x 68". $3,500.00 – 3,800.00.

Gustav Stickley inlaid maple dresser (model 911), with pivoting mirror top inlaid with stylized flowers in fruitwoods and copper, four drawers, brass knobs, and arched toeboard. Original finish, decal and paper label, 32¾" x 48" x 22". Mirror size, 33" x 40". $14,000.00+.

Not Shown

625 Dresser, 2 half drawers over 2 full, faceted pulls, 42" x 22" x 64", VG, large red decal, signed, $4,250.00 – 4,750.00.

905 Dresser, 2 drawers over 3, 33" x 48" x 23", VG, $2,000.00.

905 Dresser, 5 drawers, strap iron hardware, 48" x 23" x 58", EX, red decal, $7,000.00.

911 Dresser, iron V-pulls, original finish, 48" x 22" x 67", EX, black decal, signed, $11,000.00.

911 Dresser, 2 drawers over 2, wooden knobs, 66" x 45" x 22", EX, red decal, $2,600.00 – 2,800.00.

911, Dresser, with mirror, 2 half drawers over 2 full, 67" x 48" x 23", EX, signed, $7,000.00.

913 Dresser, V-pulls, original finish, 36" x 20" x 51", EX, branded signature, $14,000.00.

907 Vanity, 5 drawers, large mirror w/butterfly joints on harp, 48" x 22" x 55", EX, red decal, paper label, $3,000.00.

914 Vanity, 2 drawers w/wooden knobs, arched design, 36" x 18" x 54", VG, red decal, $6,000.00.

919 Vanity, 2 drawers, swivel mirror, 52½" x 36", EX, $3,500.00.

Not Shown

919 Bed, spindled, slots in headboard, 36" x 56" x 44", VG, red decal, $3,500.00.

342 Chair, two horizontal slats to back, 24" h, G, $400.00 – 450.00.

344 Chair, 3 horizontal slats to back, 26" h, VG, $550.00.

921 Dresser, 2 small drawers over 2 large, 36" x 16" x 52", EX, red decal, $3,000.00.

305 Rocker, ladder-back, 3 horizontal slats to back, 16" x 23" x 30", VG, $450.00 – 500.00.

343 Rocker, 16" x 23" x 30", VG, $260.00.

343 Rocker, 3 horizontal slats to back, 18" x 14" x 25", EX, red decal, $850.00.

343 Rocker, 3 slats to back, leather seat, 18" x 16" x 25", G, branded signature, $375.00.

215 Settle, maple, 2 slats to back, 42" x 14" x 30", VG, red decal, $3,250.00.

640 Table, tenon construction, rectangular top, 28" x 18", VG, red decal, $1,200.00.

658 Table, circular top, cross stretcher base, 24" x 20", VG, red decal, $750.00 – 1,000.00.

920 Wardrobe, iron V-pulls, paneled doors, 33" x 16½" x 60", VG, paper label, $4,675.00.

Gustav Stickley child's arm rocker (model 343). Good condition. $575.00.

Gustav Stickley rare china cabinet (model 803), designed by Harvey Ellis, with overhanging top, glass door with hammered-copper V-pull, three shelves, and arched apron. Branded Craftsman label, original finish key. Excellent condition, 60" x 36" x 15". $10,000.00.

Gustav Stickley 2-door china cabinet (model 815), with gallery top, eight panes to each door, hammered-copper V-pulls, and excellent new finish. Branded mark, paper label, 64" x 41" x 15". $6,000.00.

Gustav Stickley single-door china cabinet (model 820), with overhanging top, backsplash, 12-pane glass door with 4-pane glass side panels, and hammered-copper V-pull. Paper label and branded mark, very good original finish and condition, 63" x 36" x 14". $6,000.00.

Gustav Stickley single-door china cabinet, with backsplash, overhanging top, 12 glass panes to door, and iron V-Pull. Red decal, very good original finish, 62¾" x 36" x 15". $5,250.00.

Gustav Stickley 2-door china cabinet, with gallery top, eight panes per door, hammered-copper V-pulls, and new finish. Very good condition, 64" x 61½" x 15". $5,500.00.

Gustav Stickley single-door china cabinet (model 820), with 12 panes, backsplash, and V-shaped iron pulls. Branded mark and paper label, excellent original finish and condition, 62¾" x 36" x 15". $9,000.00.

Gustav Stickley single-door china cabinet, with 16 glass panes to door and four to each side, three fixed interior shelves, and top and base mortised through the sides. Overcoated original finish, Craftsman paper label and branded mark, very good condition, 57¾" x 35" x 13". $5,500.00.

Not Shown

955 Buffet, 2 drawers, open shelf, faceted wooden pulls, 60" x 24" x 44", VG, red decal, $15,000.00.

803 China Cabinet, single arched door over arched toeboard, 6" x 15" x 60", G, Eastwood paper label, $4,000.00.

815 China Cabinet, 2 doors w/8 panes of glass, 8 panes to side, 39" x 15" x 64", EX, red decal, $9,500.00.

815 China Cabinet, iron V-pulls on doors, 3 adjustable shelves, 40" x 15" x 64", EX, red decal, $7,000.00.

820 China Cabinet, single door w/12 panes, 4 panes to each side, 36" x 60", EX, $4,500.00.

820 China Cabinet, single door w/12 panes, backsplash, 62¾" x 36" x 15", EX, branded mark, $9,000.00.

972 China Cabinet, double doors w/24 panes, 45" x 25" x 70", EX, red decal, $24,000.00.

China Cabinet, 2 doors w/8 panes each, 36" x 14" x 56", EX, red decal, $4,750.00.

China Cabinet, single door w/16 glass panes, 4 panes to each side, 36" x 13" x 59", EX, branded signature, $5.500.00.

China Cabinet, single door w/mitered mullions, 36" x 14" x 67", VG, red decal, signed, $24,000.00.

China Cabinet, 2 glass doors, 40" x 14" x 60", G, paper label, $850.00.

China Cabinet, double doors w/8 panes to each, 42" x 16" x 63", EX, branded signature, $8,500.00.

China Cabinet, double doors w/24 panes, 52" x 15" x 64", EX, red decal, $10,000.00.

China Cabinet, single door w/16 glass panes, 57¾" x 35¼" x 13", VG, Craftsman label, $5,500.00.

China Cabinet, 2 doors, gallery top, 8 panes per door, 64¼" x 61½" x 15", VG, $5,500.00.

Gustav Stickley round oak dining table, with two leaves. Refinished, average condition, 29" x 48". $1,500.00.
Photo courtesy of Craftsman Auctions.

Gustav Stickley split-pedestal dining table, with four legs, mortised arched stretchers, and three leaves. Original finish, branded mark, excellent condition, 28½" x 48". $6,500.00.

Gustav Stickley round oak dining table (model 656). Original finish, branded, very good condition, 29½" x 54". $3,000.00 – 3,500.00. *Photo courtesy of Craftsman Auctions.*

Gustav Stickley 5-legged dining table, with circular top, apron, and four leaves. Refinished, mid-period, red decal on center leg. Very good condition, 29½" x 48". $3,500.00.

Gustav Stickley clip-corner drop-leaf table, with side stretchers and new finish. Very good condition, 30" x 42" x 14". $1,300.00.

Gustav Stickley drop-leaf dining table, with clip-corner top, new finish, and Craftsman paper label. Fair condition, 30¼" x 40" x 42". $1,300.00.

Gustav Stickley drop-leaf table, refinished, unsigned. Good condition, 30" x 42" x 40½". $1,200.00 – 1,500.00.
Photo Courtesy of Craftsman Auctions.

Gustav Stickley 5-legged drop-leaf extension dining table, with circular top and apron and four 12" leaves with holder. Original finish, very good condition, 30¾" x 48". $3,750.00.

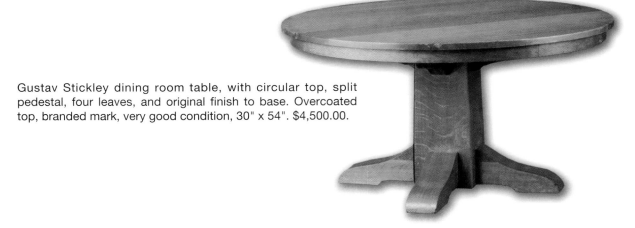

Gustav Stickley dining room table, with circular top, split pedestal, four leaves, and original finish to base. Overcoated top, branded mark, very good condition, 30" x 54". $4,500.00.

Gustav Stickley split-pedestal dining table, with circular top, shoe feet, original finish to base, and branded mark. Very good condition, 30" x 54". $4,000.00.

Gustav Stickley square oak dining room table, with two leaves, original finish, and paper label. Excellent condition. $2,875.00.
Photo courtesy of Craftsman Auctions.

Gustav Stickley 5-legged dining table, with circular top, apron, tapering posts, and seven leaves. Excellent finish, first paper label, very good condition, 54" diameter. $4,250.00.

Not Shown

418 Dining Table, 59" x 30", VG, $7,500.00.

629 Dining Table, circular top, 48" x 30", VG, $1,800.00.

632 Dining Table, 2 leaves, 48" x 29", VG, red decal, $3,750.00.

632 Dining Table, circular top, 5 legs, 6 leaves, 48" x 30", EX, red decal, signed, $5,000.00.

633 Dining Table, circular top, 5 legs, 7 leaves, 60" x 28½", VG, red decal, signed, $6,000.00.

634 Dining Table, circular top, tenon construction, 5 leaves, 53½" x 28", EX, red decal, $13,000.00.

634 Dining Table, 6 leaves, original finish, 54" x 29", EX, red decal, $15,000.00.

634 Dining Table, center leg, through-tenons, 2 leaves, 54" x 30", EX, paper label, branded, $6,000.00.

634 Dining Table, refinished top, 3 leaves, 60" x 29", VG, branded signature, $7,000.00.

647 Lunch Table, rectangular top, vertical lower stretcher, 40" x 28" x 29", VG, red decal, signed, $1,600.00.

656 Dining Table, 5 leaves, original finish, 48" x 30", VG, $2,500.00.

656 Dining Table, round top, flared pedestal base, 4 leaves, 54" x 29", VG, decal, paper label, $6,500.00.

673 Dining Table, drop leaf, 43" x 14" x 30", VG, $1,200.00.

Dining Table, circular top, pedestal base, 48" x 30", G, paper label, branded signature, $2,000.00.

Dining Table, circular top, 2 leaves, 48" x 32", VG, branded signature, $2,400.00.

Dining Table, 4 leaves, corbeled base, 54" dia., VG, branded signature, $2,200.00.

Dining Table, square top, cross stretcher base, 54" x 29", VG, $6,500.00.

Set of six Gustav Stickley dining chairs, one armchair and five side chairs, with three vertical backslats on each and upholstered seats. Armchair is covered in leather, side chairs in vinyl. Original finish. Branded marks on side chairs, red decal on armchair. Fair condition. Armchair size, 39½" x 24½" x 19". $3,000.00.

Set of eight Gustav Stickley ladder-back dining chairs, with four backslats, clond-lift aprons, drop-in seats. Recovered in leather, with overcoat. Red decal, good condition, 37" x 18" x 17". $5,500.00.

Not Shown

306 Dining Chair, ladder-back design, 3 slats to back, 36" x 17" x 17", EX, signed, $6,000.00.

306½ Dining Chair, leather seat, original finish, 36" x 17" x 16½", VG, paper label, $1,897.00.

308 Dining Chairs (set of 4), H-back, refinished, 17" x 16" x 40", G, $1,100.00.

310½ Dining Chairs (pair), original finish, 17" x 16" x 40", VG, red decal, signed, $850.00.

312½ Dining Chairs (set of 6), original finish, 22" x 18" x 37", EX, red decal, 4 signed, $4,250.00.

314 Dining Chair, leather seat, original finish, 22" x 18" x 37", EX, branded signature, $950.00.

338 Dining Chairs (pair), 3 vertical slats to back, refinished, G, $375.00.

338 Dining Chairs (pair), 16" x 21" x 40", EX, red decal, $2,400.00.

348 Dining Chairs (set of 8), 1904, ladder-back design, rush seat, 15½" x 15" x 34½", VG, early box decal, $1,500.00 – 2,000.00.

349½ Dining Chairs (pair), leather seat, 19" x 17" x 37", VG, red decal, signed, $1,100.00.

352 Dining Chairs (set of 6), drop-in seat, original finish, 18" x 16" x 37", EX, red decal, $6,000.00.

353 Dining Chair, original finish, 25" x 22" x 41", VG, red decal, signed, $800.00.

354 Dining Chairs (set of 7), leather seat, 26" x 21" x 36", EX, red decal, $10,000.00.

354½ Dining Chair (pair), leather seat, 26" x 21" x 36", VG, branded signature, $1,100.00.

357 Dining Chairs (set of 4), 36" x 18" x 16½", VG, $2,760.00.

370 Dining Chairs (set of 6), 5 sidechairs and 1 armchair, EX, red decal, signed, $2,700.00.

1296-A Dining Chair, armchair w/ arched lower front rail, 27" x 23" x 37", VG, red box, signed, $600.00.

1297 Dining Chair, early, 18" x 16" x 37", VG, red decal, $800.00.

1299 Dining Chairs (set of 6), 2 armchairs, 21" x 22" x 36", and 4 side chairs, 18" x 18" x 35", EX, red decal, signed, $24,000.00.

1301 Dining Chair (set of 6), 3 horizontal slats to back, 18" x 17" x 38", EX, red box mark, $3,250.00.

1304 Dining Chairs (pair), leather seat, original finish, 19" x 16" x 36", EX, red box mark, $2,000.00.

1304-A Dining Chairs (set of 8), horizontal slats to back, leather seat, 19" x 16" x 36", EX, red box mark, $5,500.00.

1304-A Dining Chairs (pair), armchairs, leather seat, 19" x 16" x 36", EX, red box mark, $2,000.00.

2618 Dining Chairs (set of 4), leather seat, original finish, 16" x 35", VG, red box mark, $1,300.00.

306½ Dining Chairs (set of 4), FR, $1,725.00.

306½ Dining Chairs (set of 6), 36" x 17" x 17", G, signed, $2,450.00.

Side Chairs

Set of four Gustav Stickley ladder-back side chairs (model 306½), with original leather seats over webbed support, and broad stretchers. Two are marked. Excellent condition, 36" x 16" x 19". $1,000.00.

Gustav Stickley curly maple side chair, with old refinish and original rush seat. Fair condition, 40" x 17" x 17½". $3,250.00.

Gustav Stickley V-back side chair (model 354), original leather. Good condition, 36" x 18½" x 16½". $1,100.00. *Photo courtesy of Craftsman Auctions.*

Gustav Stickley leather-back side chair (model 356), with original finish with light overcoat and replaced leather. Signed, above average condition, 37" x 19½" x 18½". $800.00. *Photo courtesy of Craftsman Auctions.*

Gustav Stickley V-back sidechair (model 354½), with small repair to lower back rail at slat, socket, original finish, original tacks with replaced leather, and early signature. Good condition, 36" x 18½" x 16½". $1,100.00. *Photo courtesy of Craftsman Auctions.*

Set of six Gustav Stickley ladder-back side chairs, upholstered in original dark brown japanned leather, with faceted tacks, original finish, some wear to edge, branded mark, and Craftsman paper label. Excellent condition, 36¼" x 17" x 17½". $4,500.00.

Gustav Stickley H-back side chair, with drop-in seat recovered in burgundy leather, overcoated original dark finish, and red decal. Good condition, 40" x 17" x 16". $600.00.

Set of four Gustav Stickley ladder-back side chairs, reupholstered in tan leather, with faceted tacks, original finish, some wear to legs, and branded mark. Very good condition, 36¼" x 17" x 17½". $1,900.00.

Gustav Stickley H-back side chair, with original seat cushion. Fair condition, 39" x 16½" x 14½". $425.00.

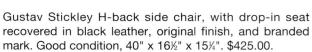

Gustav Stickley H-back side chair, with drop-in seat recovered in black leather, original finish, and branded mark. Good condition, 40" x 16½" x 15¼". $425.00.

Gustav Stickley ladder-back side chair, with new leather seat replacing the original rush. Refinished, good condition, 34" x 15" x 17". $200.00.

Set of six Gustav Stickley ladder-back side chairs, with inset dark brown leather seat pads, original finish, and red decal. Very good condition, 35¾" x 17" x 17". $6,000.00.

Gustav Stickley ladder-back side chair, with four back slats and drop-in seat cushion, that has been reupholstered in brown leather. Original finish, 1902 – 1904 decal, good condition, 37" x 18½" x 21". $500.00.

Gustav Stickley rare tall-back side chair, with three vertical slats inlaid with metal and fruitwoods in a stylized floral motiff. Inset rush seat, red decal, excellent condition, 39" x 17¼" x 16¾". $4,000.00.

Gustav Stickley ladder-back side chair, with woven rush seat and branded mark. Fair condition, 36" x 17" x 17". $325.00.

Not Shown

306 Side Chairs (pair), 3 horizontal slats to back, 17" x 17" x 36", VG, $700.00.

349 Side Chairs (set of 4), heavy ladder-back, rush seat, EX, $3,000.00.

349½ Side Chair, ladder-back, 3 horizontal slats to back, 19" x 18" x 37½", VG, red decal, signed, $1,200.00.

350 Side Chair, overcoated original finish, 40" x 17" x 16½", FR, signed, $345.00.

353 Side Chair, 3 back slats, rush seat, 30" w, G, $450.00.

353 Side Chairs (set of 6), 3 vertical slats to back, leather seats, 16" x 16" x 39", VG, $3,250.00.

370 Side Chairs (set of 3) and 370 Armchair, 35" x 17" x 16½". All FR, signed, $1,610.00.

378 Side Chair, 9 vertical spindles at back, 5 at side, 17" x 15" x 40", EX, red decal, signed, $3,500.00.

396 Side Chair, high back, with notched top rail, deep seat, 29" x 30" x 43", EX, $1,800.00.

398 Side Chair, short straight back, with drop-in seat, 16" x 16" x 33", EX, $1,400.00.

1299 Side Chair, 2 back slats, 36" w, G, $800.00.

1301 Side Chairs (pair), 3 horizontal slats, rush seat, G, $750.00.

Side Chair, Thorndew, raised pegs, 18" x 17" x 35", VG, $350.00.

Side Chair, ladder-back, 3 wide slats to back, 18" x 17" x 38", VG, red box, signed, $180.00.

Side Chair, V-back, 5 vertical back slats, 35½" x 18½" x 17", G, red decal, $1,100.00.

Side Chair, V-back, 5 vertical backslats, 35½" x 18½" x 17", G, branded mark, signed, $1,200.00.

Side Chair, V-back, 5 vertical backslats, 35½" x 18¾" x 19", G, paper label, $1,100.00.

Side Chairs (set of 2), ladder-back, woven rush seats, 36" x 17" x 17", FR, red decal, $650.00.

Side Chairs (set of 6), ladder-back, 36" x 17" x 17", G, red decal, $3,000.00.

Side Chair (pair), ladder-back, original finish, 36" x 17" x 18", FR, red decal, $650.00.

Side Chair, spindled, leather drop-in seat, 45½" x 19¼" x 17¾", G, $800.00.

Gustav Stickley 2-drawer server, designed by Harvey Ellis, with backsplash, riveted iron pulls, arched apron, lower shelf, and red decal. Very good condition, 40" x 42" x 18". $3,750.00.

Gustav Stickley rare server, with backsplash, three small drawers over one large, riveted hammered-copper oval pulls, and lower shelf. Refinished, marked, very good condition, 39¼" x 48" x 19¾". $2,600.00.

Gustav Stickley server, with backsplash, three small drawers over a linen drawer, riveted hammered-copper oval pulls, lower shelf, original finish, and red decal. Very good condition, 39¼" x 48" x 20". $3,500.00.

Gustav Stickley server, of Harvey Ellis design and with original finish on top and base. Signed, excellent condition, 43" x 54" x 21". $9,775.00. *Photo courtesy of Craftsman Auctions.*

Not Shown

802 Server, 1907, 2 short drawers, inset backsplash, 39" x 42", EX, $3,000.00.

802 Server, 2 drawers, copper pulls, tapered legs, 42" x 18" x 40", VG, red decal, $1,900.00.

818 Server, 3 drawers, oval iron pulls, 48" x 20" x 39", VG, red decal, $3,250.00.

819 Server, 3 drawers, oval iron pulls, lower shelf, 48" x 20" x 39", VG, signed, $4,250.00.

962 Server, 3 drawers, faceted wooden pulls, chamfered sides, 60" x 16" x 37", VG, $17,000.00.

970 Server, early, double-keyed tenons, iron hardware, 44" x 20" x 37", EX, $7,000.00.

Server, double-keyed tenons, lower shelf, 42" x 21" x 33", EX, $9,000.00.

Server, rare, plate rail, tenon construction, 44¼" x 59" x 29", VG, red decal, $35,000.00.

Server, 2 short drawers over 1 long, 48" x 20" x 44", VG, red decal, $1,600.00.

20 Server Tray, 20" diameter, hammered-copper, G, Craftsman stamp, $700.00 – 1,000.00.

Server Trays (pair), copper, circular, 11¼" x 11", G, stamped "Als Ik Kan," $600.00.

Sideboards

Gustav Stickley sideboard (model 814½), with original finish, three small drawers flanked by two cabinets, and one large drawer. Red decal, signed, very good condition, 56" x 22" x 48". $7,000.00. *Photo courtesy of Craftsman Auctions.*

Gustav Stickley sideboard, with a linen drawer over three smaller drawers and two cabinets, plate rail, and excellent original finish. Red decal and paper label, very good condition, 41½" x 48" x 18". $4,250.00. *Photo courtesy of Craftsman Auctions.*

Gustav Stickley sideboard, with plate rail, linen drawer over two cabinets and three center drawers, arched apron, and original finish. Decal and paper label, very good condition, 45" x 48" x 18". $3,750.00 – 4,750.00.

Gustav Stickley sideboard, with plate rail with arched top, two cabinets with hammered-copper strap hinges and hardware, three center drawers, and a linen drawer. Refinished, branded mark, excellent condition, 48" x 56" x 22". $3,500.00.

Gustav Stickley 8-legged sideboard, with chamfered plate rack, four drawers with faceted wooden pulls, and two doors with hammered-copper hardware. Refinished, very good condition, 49" x 69½" x 25". $9,500.00.

Gustav Stickley 8-legged sideboard, with paneled back, plate rail, and four drawers flanked by cabinets with riveted hammered-copper strap hinges. Refinished, paper label in drawer, excellent condition, 50" x 70" x 24¼". $7,500.00.

Gustav Stickley 8-legged sideboard, with paneled back, plate rail, four center drawers flanked by cabinets with interior shelves, and riveted hammered-copper strap hinges and drop pulls. Refinished, patina loss to hardware, very good condition, 50" x 70" x 25½". $6,000.00.

Gustav Stickley sideboard, with three center drawers and two cabinet doors over a linen drawer, and original hammered-copper pulls. Good condition, 38" x 56" x 21½". $1,100.00.

Gustav Stickley sideboard, with plate rail, linen drawer over two cabinets and three center drawers, and arched apron. Decal and paper label, very good condition, 45" x 48" x 18". $3,750.00 – 4,000.00.

Gustav Stickley sideboard, with plate rail, linen drawer, and three center drawers flanked by cabinets. Refinished, plate rail attached to top. Paper label & branded mark, very good condition, 45" x 48" x 18½". $3,500.00.

Gustav Stickley sideboard, with linen drawer over two small drawers, open cubbyhole, two cabinets, brass drop pulls, original finish, Craftsman paper label, and red decal. Very good condition, 45½" x 48½" x 18¼". $3,000.00.

Gustav Stickley sideboard (model 814), with plate rail, three center drawers flanked by cabinets, linen drawer, iron drop pulls, strap hardware, original finish, and branded mark. Very good condition, 43¼" x 56" x 22¼". $3,250.00.

Gustav Stickley sideboard, with linen drawer over three small drawers and two cabinets, and hammered-copper drop pulls. Refinished, branded mark, very good condition, 45¼" x 48" x 18½". $3,500.00 – 4,500.00.

Not Shown

814 Sideboard, tenon construction, 2 cabinet doors, 3 half drawers, 66" x 24" x 49", EX, red decal, $7,000.00.

814½ Sideboard, 3 drawers over 1, 56" x 49" x 22", EX, burned mark, $6,000.00.

816 Sideboard, 1 long drawer over 3 short, 48" x 19" x 46", VG, $2,100.00.

817 Sideboard, 8 legs with iron hardware, 70" x 26" x 50", EX, Eastwood label, $6,500.00.

1301 Sideboard, 8 legs, 4 drawers, copper straps, 70" x 25" x 50", VG, red decal, signed, $8,000.00.

Sideboard, overhanging rectangular top, 3 drawers, 38" x 56" x 22", FR, branded, $1,300.00.

Armchairs

Gustav Stickley armchair (model 2632), with horizontal backslats. Refinished, very good condition, 37" x 27" x 22". $690.00.

Gustav Stickley V-back armchair, and with vertical backslats and replaced leather seat with original faceted tacks. Good original finish and condition, red decal, 37" x 26" x 20½". $900.00.

Gustav Stickley armchair, with five vertical backslats, replaced seat support, loose fabric cushion, original finish, and red decal. Good condition, 37" x 27" x 25". $650.00.

Early Gustav Stickley V-back armchair, with five vertical slats, corbels, tacked-on original leather seat, excellent original dark finish, normal wear on top of arms, and small tears to leather. Early box mark, excellent condition, 36" x 26" x 20". $900.00.

Gustav Stickley armchair (model 320), with five vertical slats under flat arms and on the back, red leather, and covered seat. Good condition, 38" x 21" x 23". $550.00.

Gustav Stickley armchair, with four vertical backslats, open arms, long corbels, new tan leather-upholstered seat cushion, and conjoined symbols decal. Very good condition, 39" x 26½" x 23". $450.00.

Gustav Stickley fixed-back armchair (model 324), with slats to seat rail, corbels under the arms, new brown leather loose cushions, and original finish with overcoat. Very good condition, 41" x 29" x 31". $1,800.00.

Gustav Stickley ladder-back armchair, with five short vertical slats to each side, red velvet-upholstered cushions, worn original finish, loose glue joints, and signature inside seat rail. Fair condition, 31" x 29" x 31". $1,100.00.

Early Gustav Stickley ladder-back armchair, with scooped crestrail, cloudlift apron, wooven cane seat, excellent original dark finish, and red decal. Excellent condition, 39" x 23" x 21". $4,000.00.

Early Gustav Stickley ladder-back armchair, with scooped crestrail, cloudlift apron, woven cane seat, fine original dark finish, several splits to caning, and red decal. Fair condition, 39" x 23" x 21". $2,400.00.

Gustav Stickley H-back armchair (model 314), refinished, with replaced leather. Branded, average condition, 39½" x 25" x 21". $700.00. *Photo courtesy of Craftsman Auctions.*

Early Gustav Stickley ladder-back armchair, with scooped top rail, new Cordovan leather cushions on woven jute seat support, good original finish, and box decal. Good condition, 37" x 26¾" x 25". $1,300.00.

Gustav Stickley tall-back armchair, with spindles to back and sides, and dark brown leather uphostered cushion. Refinished, red decal, excellent condition, 49" x 27" x 22". $3,500.00.

Gustav Stickley armchair, with three vertical backslats, tacked-on brown leather seat, overcoat to original finish, some loss of color, and red decal. Very good condition, 38¼" x 26¼" x 22½". $600.00.

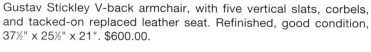

Gustav Stickley V-back armchair, with five vertical slats, corbels, and tacked-on replaced leather seat. Refinished, good condition, 37½" x 25½" x 21". $600.00.

Gustav Stickley cube chair, with spindled back and sides, cushions reupholstered in new dark brown leather, excellent new finish, and decal. Excellent condition, 29" x 25¾" x 27½". $8,500.00.

Gustav Stickley V-back armchair, with vertical slats, corbels, tacked-on leather seat, original dark finish, and early box mark. Excellent condition, 36" x 26" x 20". $900.00.

Not Shown

310½ Armchair, 25" x 21" x 36", G, red decal, $475.00.

310½ Armchairs (pair), heavy ladder-back form, 27" x 22" x 36", VG, red decal, $1,400.00.

310½ Armchair, ladder-back, open arms, 37¼" x 26½" x 22", FR, $500.00.

312½ Armchair, leather seat, original finish, 22" x 18" x 37", VG, $450.00.

316 Armchair, inverted V-back, open arms, 23" x 19½" x 37", VG, $500.00.

318 Armchair, 5 slats to back, 27" x 23" x 37", VG, $500.00.

320 Armchair, original finish, 29" x 29" x 42", EX, red decal, $1,200.00.

320 Armchair, four horizontal slats to back, 29" x 31" x 41", EX, red decal, signed, $1,800.00.

326 Armchair, rope seat, 5 slats to back, 24½" x 20½" x 37", EX, red decal, $550.00.

328 Armchair, single wide slat to sides & back, refinished, 26" x 28" x 28", VG, $3,000.00.

335 Armchair (cube), 29" x 26" x 28", VG, $4,887.00.

344 Armchair (child's), 3 slats to back, 18" x 14" x 26", VG, red decal, $375.00.

353-A, Armchair (pair), 3 slats to back, drop-in seat, 25" x 21" x 41", VG, $1,800.00 – 2,000.00.

354-A Armchair, V-back, 5 slats to back, 26" x 21" x 36", EX, red decal, signed, $1,500.00.

354 Armchair, V-back, 35½" x 26" x 20½", $575.00.

354½ Armchair, V-back, 36" x 26" x 20½", AVG, signed, $800.00 – 1,000.00.

366 Armchair (pair), 3 vertical slats to back, leather seat, 26" x 22" x 39", VG, red decal, signed, $1,400.00.

391 Armchair, spring cushion, original finish, 26" x 28" x 29", EX, red decal, $24,000.00.

396 Armchair, refinished, 32" x 33" x 40", VG, branded, $2,800.00.

2590 Armchair, early, V-back, 5 slats to back, open arms, 26" x 21" x 38", EX, red decal, $2,200.00.

2590 Armchair, 4 horizontal slats to back, open arms, 31" x 29" x 39", EX, red decal, $3,000.00.

2603 Armchair, arched top over 3 horizontal slats, rope foundation, 27" x 26" x 37", VG, $400.00.

2604 Armchair, rare, curved arm, back rail, 25" x 25" x 38", VG, $2,500.00.

Armchairs (pair), soled seat, keyed tenon construction, refinished, 23" x 18" x 40", VG, 1 signed w/red decal, $850.00.

Armchair, double horizontal rail above 3 slats, refinished, 24" x 21" x 44", VG, $8,000.00.

Armchair, arched seat rails on all 4 sides, refinished, 29" x 31" x 40", VG, early box mark, $3,000.00.

Armchair, w/vertical backslats, 37½" x 27½" x 22", G, $862.00.

Gustav Stickley spindle-back slipper chair, with drop-in new green leather seat and original finish. Good condition, 32½" x 17" x 16". $850.00.

Early Gustav Stickley rare spindle-back slipper chair, with drop-in spring seat recovered in brown leather, good original finish, and black decal. Very good condition, 37" x 17¾" x 16". $1,000.00.

Gustav Stickley slipper chair, with laced brown hard leather seat, footrest with corbeled supports and stretchers, original finish and leather, and metal brackets under footrest. Branded, good condition, 24½" x 15½" x 15". $475.00.

Not Shown

353, Chairs (set of 7), mahogany, rush seats, 17" x 17" x 40", G, red decal, signed, $3,250.00.

Chair, H-back, drop-in seat, 17" x 16" x 40", VG, $400.00.

Chair (cube), rare, slats to back & sides, 26" x 28" x 28", VG, $140,000.00.

Chair (slipper), spindled, original finish, 32½" x 16" x 17", EX, signed, $1,500.00 – 2,000.00.

Chair (slipper), spindled back, chair, drop-in seat, 32½" x 17" x 15", FR, $160.00 – 200.00.

Chair (slipper), H-shaped backslat, 35½" x 16¾" x 15½", FR, branded signature, $250.00.

Clocks

Not Shown

Clock (mantle), through-tenon construction, 8½" x 5" x 14", EX, Signed, $6,000.00.

Clock (mantle), face w/company logo behind door, EX, $8,000.00.

Gustav Stickley rare oak shelf clock, with original finish and branded signature. Excellent condition. 14" x 8½" x 5". $9,200.00. *Photo courtesy of Craftsman Auctions.*

Gustav Stickley flat-arm Morris chair (model 332), with vertical side slats, long corbels under the arms, and blue velvet-upholstered cushion. Refinished, very good condition, 40" x 31" x 38". $5,000.00 – 7,000.00.

Early Gustav Stickley flat-arm Morris chair (model 332), with slats to the floor and original brown woven fabric tufted cushions. Excellent original finish and condition, full box decal (rare), 40" x 31½" x 36⅓". $14,000.00 – 19,000.00.

Gustav Stickley open-arm Morris chair, with trapezoidal arms, corbels, and new leather drop-in cushion on wood slat foundation. Good original finish and condition, Eastwood label, 39" x 30" x 32½". $2,500.00.

Gustav Stickley bow-arm Morris Chair, with recaned seat support and reupholstered tan leather seat and back cushions. Very good condition, 36" x 34" x 36½". $14,000.00.

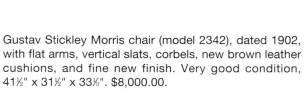

Gustav Stickley Morris chair (model 2342), dated 1902, with flat arms, vertical slats, corbels, new brown leather cushions, and fine new finish. Very good condition, 41½" x 31½" x 33⅓". $8,000.00.

Early Gustav Stickley rare Morris chair (model 2341), 1902 – 1904 era, with four horizontal backslats, corbeled sides, and two vertical slats. Red decal, very good condition, 38" x 29½" x 33⅓". $4,500.00.

Gustav Stickley Morris chair, with spindled sides, long corbels under flat arms, new green leather cushions, good new finish, and front stretcher. Very good condition, 40" x 30" x 36". $4,500.00.

Gustav Stickley drop-arm Morris chair, recovered in green leather, with drop-in spring seat, loose pillow, overcoated original finish, and branded mark. Very good condition, 38¾" x 32½" x 37½". $9,500.00.

Gustav Stickley Morris chair (model 332), with slats under flat arms, drop-in spring seat, and replaced leather seat. Refinished, replaced pins, good condition, 41" x 31" x 40". $4,750.00.

Gustav Stickley Morris chair (model 332), with original finish and early box signature. Excellent condition, 39" x 32" x 36". $11,000.00 – 12,000.00. *Photo courtesy of Craftsman Auctions.*

Not Shown

319 Morris Chair, open under arms, 31" x 34" x 39", G, red decal, $1,100.00.

332 Morris Chair, 5 slats under arms, pegs, 32" x 36" x 40", VG, red decal, signed, $6,250.00 – 8,500.00.

332 Morris Chair, 5 wide slats under flat arms, faceted pegs, 32" x 38" x 40", VG, $6,250.00.

332 Morris Chair, 39" x 32" x 36", EX, early box signature, $11,000.00 – 14,000.00.

369 Morris Chair, 40" x 33" x 37½", VG, $8,000.00.

333 Morris Chair, 7 slats under each arm, 29" x 31" x 38", VG, branded signature, $4,250.00.

334 Morris Chair, leather seat, copper tacks front & back, 37" x 30" x 33", VG, 1904 decal, $3,500.00 – 3,750.00.

334 Morris Chair, 38" x 29" x 33", EX, early signature, $5,000.00 – 6,000.00.

336 Morris Chair, arched seat support, cane foundation, 30" x 36" x 39", EX, $12,000.00.

336 Morris Chair, bow arms, pegs, 30" x 36" x 42", VG, branded signature, $7,500.00.

336 Morris Chair, leather cushions, 30" x 36" x 44", VG, $4,750.00.

346 Morris Chair, open arms, 30" x 33" x 42", EX, red decal, $3,500.00.

366 Morris Chair, EX, $12,000.00.

346 Morris Chair, original finish, 31" x 34" x 42", EX, $2,000.00.

367 Morris Chair, 1904, spindles under arms, 27" x 34" x 38", EX, signed decal, $12,000.00.

367 Morris Chair, 17 spindles under flat arms, refinished, 30" x 36" x 39", VG, paper label, $7,500.00.

367 Morris Chair, bow arms, 37" x 30" x 36", EX, $11,000.00.

367 Morris Chair, 18 spindles, replaced pegs, 40" h, EX, $11,550.00.

369 Morris Chair, 5 vertical slats under arms, 24" x 40", VG, $8,000.00.

369 Morris Chair, 5 vertical slats, 33" x 38" x 38", EX, red decal, branded signature, $12,000.00 – 18,000.00.

369 Morris Chair, 16 slats under bent arms, tenon construction, 33" x 38" x 39", VG, $8,500.00.

369 Morris Chair, slant arms, slats under arms, 33" x 38" x 40", VG, branded signature, $6,500.00.

2340 Morris Chair, early, bow arms, tapered legs, 28" x 33" x 41", EX, $47,500.00.

2340 Morris Chair, early, narrow arms, tapered legs, 29" x 33" x 39", VG. $6,500.00 – 8,000.00.

2340 Morris Chair, early, reverse-taper bow arm, 39" x 28½" x 33", EX, $12,650.00.

2341 Morris Chair, 2 slats, interior corbels under each arm, 29" x 34" x 38", VG, $3,000.00.

2341 Morris Chair, 2 vertical slats under each arm, 30" x 34" x 37", EX, $10,000.00.

Rockers

Gustav Stickley open-arm rocker, with five vertical slats to back, reupholstered tan leather seat cushion, original finish, and added brackets under arms. Red decal, very good condition, 37½" x 27½" x 26⅓". $1,000.00.

Gustav Stickley V-back rocker, with five vertical backslats, open arms, green vinyl-covered seat, and original finish. Fair condition, 35" x 26" x 24". $600.00.

Gustav Stickley open-arm rocker, with seat and back cushions recovered in green leather. Refinished, very good condition, 40½" x 29" x 33". $1,500.00 – 2,000.00.

Gustav Stickley rocker, with open arms, three vertical backslats, replaced leather upholstered seat, original finish, and red decal. Good condition, 37" x 26½" x 27". $550.00.

Gustav Stickley ladder-back rocker (model 319), with scooped crestrail, open sides, upholstered seat and back cushions, original finish, and red decal. Good condition, 38½" x 29" x 34". $1,300.00.

Gustav Stickley armchair rocker with V-crestrail, five vertical backslats, reupholstered red vinyl cushion, overcoated original finish, and red decal. Good condition, 34" x 25½" x 22". $450.00.

Not Shown

309 Rocker, 3 horizontal slats to back, open under arms, 25" x 29" x 32", G, $500.00.

309 Rocker, 3 slats, ladder-back, rush seat, 32", VG, $650.00.

309½ Rocker, 3 horizontal slats with open arms, 25" x 21" x 32", VG, red decal, $350.00 – 375.00.

309½ Rocker, ladder-back, 3 horizontal slats, 25" x 28" x 32", FR, red decal, $600.00.

311½ Rocker, mahogany, V-back, 5 vertical slats to back, 26" x 19" x 34", VG, red decal, $375.00.

311½ Rocker, mahogany, 5 vertical slats, open arms, original finish, 26" x 21" x 33", G, $425.00 – 650.00.

313 Rocker, high back, leather seat, 37", VG, $700.00.

317 Rocker, 5 vertical slats, original finish, 27" x 23" x 38", EX, red decal, $750.00 – 850.00.

319 Rocker, replaced cane foundation, original finish, 29" x 32" x 39", VG, red decal, $1,600.00.

319 Rocker, 4 horizontal slats to back, notched, top rail, 29" x 35" x 39", EX, red decal, signed, $2,400.00.

319 Rocker, open arms, corbeled front posts, 38" x 29½", VG, $700.00 – 1,000.00.

319 Rocker, 40" x 29" x 28", G, signed, $1,495.00.

323 Rocker, recovered cushion, original finish, 28" x 35" x 40", VG, $2,200.00.

323 Rocker, 5 slats under flat arms, original finish, 29" x 31" x 42", VG, $2,200.00.

323 Rocker, large, 5 wide slats under arms, cane foundation, 29" x 32" x 37", G, $1,800.00.

337 Rocker, 3 vertical slats to back, arched seat rails, 15" x 23" x 34", EX, branded signature, $500.00.

359 Rocker, worn leather seat, 26" x 21" x 37", VG, paper label, $325.00.

359-A Rocker, open arms, 11 spindles to back, leather seat, 26" x 21" x 37", VG, red decal, $1,600.00 – 1,800.00.

365 Rocker, 3 vertical slats to back, 26" x 20" x 38", VG, branded signature, $800.00.

373 Rocker, 11 spindles to back, 7 spindles each side, 19" x 18" x 42", EX, red decal, $2,500.00.

393 Rocker, high back w/5 vertical slats, 27" x 24" x 44", VG, red decal, $2,700.00.

2603 Rocker, 4 vertical slats to back, open arms, refinished, 27" x 26" x 36", VG, $450.00.

2603 Rocker, 4 vertical slats to back, open arms, 27" x 31" x 36", EX, red box mark, signed, $650.00.

2603 Rocker, early, orignal finish, 36" x 25½" x 23", EX, signed, $1,200.00 – 1,500.00.

2625 Rocker, 5 vertical slats to back, original finish, 27" x 26" x 37", EX, red decal, $750.00.

2627 Rocker, 5 curved vertical slats, 18" x 24" x 31", VG, $750.00.

2632 Rocker, 3 wide vertical slats, 27" x 29" x 39", G, $1,100.00.

Not Shown

2637 Rocker (arm), 2 wide horizontal boards to back, rush seat, 21" x 19" x 32", G, $400.00.

Rocker, Thornden, 2 wide slats to back, cane seat, 21" x 27" x 32", VG, $325.00.

Rocker, Thornden, 2 wide slats to back, single arm, 21" x 28" x 33", VG, red box mark, $3,000.00.

Rocker, 4 vertical slats to back, drop-in seat, 25" x 23" x 39", EX, $850.00.

Rocker, ladder-back, crestrail, leather seat, 33" x 26" x 23", VG, red decal, $2,000.00 – 2,500.00.

Gustav Stickley even-arm settle (model 208), with vertical slats all around, top rail mortised through the legs, and drop-in spring seat covered in new green leather. Red decal, very good condition, 29⅓" x 76½" x 32". $6,000.00.

Gustav Stickley crib settle with square posts, angled vertical slats to back and sides, new rope support, new dark finish, and corner blocks on underside. No cushion, excellent condition, 39" x 68½" x 33". $4,750.00.

Gustav Stickley V-back settle, with vertical backslats, scooped arms, original leather and tacks, and enhanced finish. Red decal and paper label, excellent condition, 36" x 47⅓" x 24". $3,000.00 – 3,500.00.

Gustav Stickley settle (model 225), with single broad horizontal back panel and vertical side slats, drop-in seat recovered in brown leather, and overcoated original finish. Very good condition, 29⅓" x 59¾" x 31". $6,500.00.

Gustav Stickley V-back settle, with vertical backslats, scooped arms, original leather and tacks, and original finish. Red decal, paper label, excellent condition, 36" x 47⅓" x 24". $3,000.00 – 3,500.00.

Gustav Stickley willow chair (model 64), with original finish. This chair was formerly exhibited at the Renwick Gallery of The Smithsonian Institution. Excellent condition, 32" x 31" x 27". $3,600.00. *Photo courtesy of Craftsman Auctions.*

Not Shown

70 Settle, willow, original finish, 90" x 30" x 33", VG, $3,750.00.

161 Settle, 4 horizontal slats to back, 50" x 27" x 38", VG, $1,800.00.

172 Settle, keyed through-tenon construction, 56" x 21" x 33", VG, $3,500.00.

173 Settle, 13 slats to back, 4 slats under arms, 71" x 29" x 39", VG, $8,500.00.

203 Settle (hall), 5 vertical slats to back, 56" x 22" x 30", G, red decal, signed, $1,800.00.

205 Settle (hall), wide slats across back & under arms, 56" x 22" x 30", VG, red decal, signed, $6,000.00.

206 Settle, 7 wide slats to back, 3 on each side, 60" x 28" x 40", EX, red decal, $12,000.00.

208 Settle, 3 slats under arms 8 to back, 77" x 32" x 29", VG, branded signature, $6,000.00.

212 Settle, 36" x 47½" x 24", $1,500.00 – 2,000.00.

212 Settle, 12 slats to back, leather seat, 47" x 25" x 36", VG, red decal, $2,400.00 – 3,750.00.

222 Settle, 22 slats to back, 8 slats under arm, 80" x 32" x 37", EX, red decal, $15,000.00.

225 Settle, 5 wide slats under even arms, 78" x 31" x 29", EX, red decal, signed, $6,500.00.

226 Settle, 5 Slats under each arm, wide back rail, 60" x 31" x 29", EX, branded signature, $7,000.00.

Footstools

Not Shown

299 Footstool, 16" x 9", EX, red decal, $600.00 – 650.00.

300 Footstool, 21" x 17" x 15", VG, red decal, $1,200.00.

301 Footstool, rush seat, 20" x 16" x 18", VG, red decal, $400.00.

302 Footstool, 12" x 12" x 15", VG, $400.00.

389 Footstool, G, $400.00.

395 Footstool, 7 spindles to each side, tenon construction, 20" x 16" x 15", VG, $3,250.00.

Footstool, spindled sides, 15" x 20" x 16", G, Signed, $1,200.00.

Footstool, rush seat, 17½" x 19½" x 15½", G, Branded mark, $350.00.

Footstool (Ellis style), 18" x 19½" x 15½", AVG+, signed, $800.00 – 1,000.00.

Not Shown

Coat Stand, 70¾" x 22", G, $1,500.00.

52 Costumer, single pole, 4 iron hooks, 27" x 72", VG, $600.00.

53 Costumer, 4 extra hooks on double-tapered pole, 13" x 72", EX, red decal, $3,250.00.

Costumer, single pole, original iron hooks, 23" x 72", VG, $500.00.

Costumer (hatrack), 71½", G, $805.00.

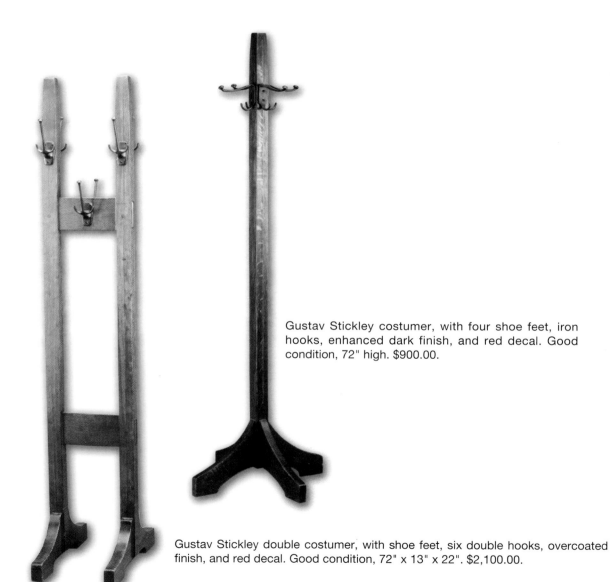

Gustav Stickley costumer, with four shoe feet, iron hooks, enhanced dark finish, and red decal. Good condition, 72" high. $900.00.

Gustav Stickley double costumer, with shoe feet, six double hooks, overcoated finish, and red decal. Good condition, 72" x 13" x 22". $2,100.00.

Gustav Stickley hall bench (model 224), with lift seat and original finish. Excellent condition. $5,000.00. *Photo courtesy of Craftsman Auction.*

Gustav Stickley gout stool, with replaced leather and good original finish. Red decal and paper label. Very good condition, 4¾" x 11¾" x 11¾". $850.00 – 1,200.00.

Early Gustav Stickley hall bench (model 180), with broad horizontal backslat, arms, keyed tenon stretcher mortised through the legs, replaced leather seat, original finish, and "Als Ik Kan" mark. Very good condition, 35½" x 41½" x 21⅓". $3,250.00.

Not Shown

182 Hall Bench, rare, 8 vertical slats to back, 48" x 26" x 37", VG, $16,000.00.

219 Hall Bench, 17 back slats, open arms w/corbels, 72" x 26" x 38", VG, $1,600.00.

224 Hall Seat, cutouts on sides, paneled back, 48" x 22" x 42", EX, branded signature, $9,000.00.

Hall Seat, heavy through-tenon construction (very rare), 24" x 18" x 28", VG, $3,000.00.

205 Hall Settle, wide slats across back & under arms, 56" x 22" x 30", VG, $2,200.00.

Window Bench, rails, mortised through the sides, 26½" x 25" x 18½", VG, $4,500.00.

177 Window Seat, V-seat, rail above keyed tenon stretchers, 25" x 19" x 26", EX, red decal, $3,250.00.

178 Window Seat, vertical through-tenon arms, 36" x 19" x 26", VG, large red decal, signed, $3,500.00.

152 Window Settle, turned legs, 25" x 19" x 30", VG, $1,400.00.

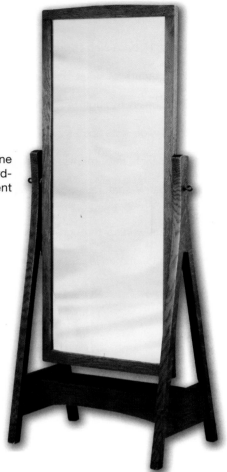

Gustav Stickley cheval mirror (model 914), with wishbone legs, arched stretchers mortised through sides, iron hardware, fine original finish, and large red decal. Excellent condition, 69" x 28" x 12". $19,000.00.

Gustav Stickley hall mirror (model 68), with fine new finish. Signed, above average condition, 28" x 42". $3,500.00.

Photo courtesy of Craftsman Auctions.

Not Shown

66 Mirror, 4 iron coat hooks, original finish, 28" x 36", EX, red decal, $2,300.00.

68 Mirror, 3 sections, 4 iron hooks, 48" x 28", VG, paper label, red decal, $1,500.00.

608 Mirror, rectangular, 42" x 29", VG, $1,500.00.

633 Mirror (wall), candle sconce, 23" x 29", G, branded signature, $1,500.00.

916 Mirror, maple, peaked top, 30" x 24", VG, red decal, signed, $1,600.00.

918 Mirror (cheval), 1904, double arch stretchers, 30" x 17" x 70", EX, red decal, $7,000.00.

Mirror, wall, arched top rail, 23½" x 29", G, branded "Stickley," signed, $1,200.00 – 1,500.00.

Mirror (wishbone), arched frame, 4' base, 26" x 20", VG, red decal, signed, $1,800.00.

Umbrella Stands

Not Shown

54 Umbrella Stand, square framed, square finials, 12" x 12" x 33", G, $500.00.

54 Umbrella Stand, recent finish, 29" h, EX, paper label, $660.00.

54 Umbrella Stand, 4 tapered posts, copper drip pan, 12" x 34", EX, red decal, $1,700.00.

55 Umbrella Stand, 4 tapered posts, divided top, 34" h, G, $850.00.

100, Umbrella Stand, flared/slatted, 12" x 24", VG, $1,800.00.

Umbrella Stand, hammered copper, 2 handles, 14" x 24", VG, signed, $4,000.00.

Umbrella Stand, 10 vertical slats, 3 iron rings, 24" h, VG, $3,250.00.

Umbrella Stand, hammered copper, tree decoration, 24" x 12½", VG, circular stamp mark, $2,800.00.

Umbrella Stand, hammered copper, tree decoration, 25" x 13", G, $1,400.00.

Umbrella Stand (triple), 34" x 21" x 12", G, $750.00.

Early Gustav Stickley rare table lamp, with faceted oak base, original wicker shade with replaced silk lining, and original acorn chain pull. Mint original condition, 16" x 10". $1,000.00.

Gustav Stickley fine and rare hammered-copper chandelier, with cross form rivited bracket, four pendant lanterns with hammered yellow glass panels, original 8'8" hanging chain and ceiling plate, and original patina and glass. "Als Ik Kan" stamped mark on ceiling plate. Excellent condition, 21" x 21½" diameter. $17,000.00.

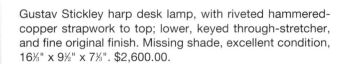

Gustav Stickley harp desk lamp, with riveted hammered-copper strapwork to top; lower, keyed through-stretcher, and fine original finish. Missing shade, excellent condition, 16⅛" x 9½" x 7⅛". $2,600.00.

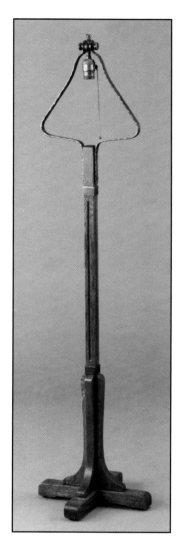

Gustav Stickley floor lamp, with hammered-copper bell-shaped harp and buttressed base, original finish, and no shade. Marked "Als Ik Kan," very good condition, 57" x 13½". $2,400.00.

Gustav Stickley floor lamp, with hammered-copper harp, quezal bell-shaped shade on a footed base, original finish and patina, and stamped mark. Very good condition, 57" x 12". $3,750.00.

Basket, wood, hammered curled-iron base, oak slats, 31" x 26" x 12", EX, $7,000.00.

26 Cabinet (smoker's), rectangular top, single drawer, 20" x 15" x 29", VG, red decal, $2,300.00.

89 Cabinet (smoker's), iron strap hardware, small drawer, 20" x 14" x 29", EX, red decal, $9,500.00.

Cabinet (liquor), paneled drop front, 26" x 14" x 52", EX, red decal, $13,000.00.

Cabinet (smoker's), 1904, 20" x 16" x 30", EX, red decal, signed, $11,000.00.

Cabinet, rectangular top over single drawer, iron hardware, 20" x 15" x 29", EX, branded signature, $2,000.00.

Cabinet (vice), dovetailed, hinged lid, 2 copper shelves, 42½" x 24" x 17", VG, Craftsman paper label, $3,750.00 – 4,750.00.

86 Cellarette, flip-top lid, with dovetail construction, 24" x 18" x 43", VG, red decal, $2,400.00.

Chest (bridal), cedar lined, paneled sides, and arched corbels, 41" x 21" x 25", EX, red box mark, $12,000.00.

Chest (bridal), double iron hardware, paneled sides, 41" x 21" x 24", VG, $6,500.00.

Dinner Gong, 24" x 10" x 37", VG, $5,000.00.

83 Screen, trifold, wooden frame, brown canvas, 66" x 67½" x 21", EX, red decal, $1,800.00.

95 Shirt-waist Box, eleven spindles to each side, 30" x 16" x 16", VG, paper label, $7,000.00.

Shirt-waist Box, through-tenons at top & bottom, 16" x 30" x 16", EX, paper label, $4,500.00.

522 Somno, early, chamfered, through tenons on all 4 sides, 17" x 15" x 27", VG, red decal, $5,000.00.

605 Somno, flat top, lower compartment, 18" x 16" x 30", EX, $7,000.00.

Washstand, 2 small drawers over 2 cabinet doors, 41" x 22" x 29", EX, red decal, $7,000.00.

Early Gustav Stickley rare somno, with single drawer, lower cabinet with paneled sides, pyramidial wooden pulls, and new finish. Excellent condition, 33½" x 19¾" x 16". $4,000.00.

Music Cabinets & Stands

Not Shown

70 Music Cabinet, single paneled door, iron hardware, 20" x 16" x 46", EX, red decal, $9,500.00.

674 Music Stand, spindled sides, 4 shelves, 20" x 14" x 42", VG, paper label, $2,900.00.

Gustav Stickley rare music cabinet, with gallery top, single door with 12 panes of hammered amber glass, adjustable interior shelves, and mint original finish. Branded mark and paper label, excellent condition, 54½" x 20" x 16". $14,000.00.

Gustav Stickley music rack (model 670), with tapered posts and four shelves bordered with backsplashes. Refinished, paper label, good condition, 39⅓" x 22" x 15". $3,750.00.

Gustav Stickley rare music cabinet, with gallery top, single door, hammered-copper V-pull, and fine original finish and condition. Branded mark and paper label, 47½" x 19¾" x 17". $5,500.00.

Gustav Stickley music cabinet (model 70), with amber glass and original finish with overcoat. Brand and paper label, excellent condition, 47½" x 19½" x 16". $7,475.00.
Photo courtesy of Craftsman Auctions.

Gustav Stickley rare single-door, mahogany bookcase, designed by Harvey Ellis, with overhanging top, pilaster posts, arched apron, two long mullions, and square leaded panes in door. Red decal, excellent condition, 57¾" x 36" x 14". $17,000.00.

Gustav Stickley single-door bookcase, with 16 glass panes, gallery top, through-tenon construction, and copper ring pull with original key. Red decal, excellent condition, 55½" x 35¾" x 12¾". $8,500.00.

Gustav Stickley double-door bookcase, with gallery top, through-tenon construction, eight glass panes per door, and hammered-copper V-pulls. Branded mark and second paper label, very good condition, 56" x 43" x 13". $7,500.00.

Gustav Stickley double-door bookcase, with gallery top, 12 panes per door, brass V-pulls, and mortised top. Refinished, paper label, good condition, 55" x 54" x 13". $4,500.00.

Gustav Stickley double-door bookcase, with original finish. Signed, average condition, 56" x 47½" x 12½". $6,000.00.
Photo courtesy of Craftsman Auctions.

Gustav Stickley double-door bookcase, with gallery top, 16 mitered and mullioned panes per door, ring pulls, three shelves per section, chamfered back, and new reddish-brown finish. Large decal, excellent condition, 56" x 61⅓". $10,000.00 – 12,000.00.

Gustav Stickley double-door bookcase, with mitered mullions, original finish, and very good color. Early box signature, above average condition, 56" x 49" x 12". $9,000.00. *Photo courtesy of Craftsman Auctions.*

Gustav Stickley double-door mahogany bookcase, Harvey Ellis. Paper label, excellent condition, 58" x 42" x 14". $7,475.00. *Photo courtesy of Craftsman Auctions.*

Gustav Stickley revolving book-rack, with original finish. Label, excellent condition, 9½" x 13". $3,392.00. *Photo courtesy of Craftsman Auctions.*

Gustav Stickley double-door bookcase, dated 1902 – 1903, with chamfered back, gallery top, keyed through-tenon construction, nine mitered and mullioned glass panes in each door, double cabinet doors, rare copper strap hardware, and fine original finish. Very good condition, large red decal, 62" x 59" x 17". This did not sell when it was presented for auction in 2002, but its estimated bid price was $75,000.00 – 100,000.00.

Early Gustav Stickley double-door mahogany bookcase, dated 1904 – 1905, designed by Harvey Ellis, with overhanging top, pilaster posts, arched apron, two long panes topped by two leaded square panes on each door, key lock, and three refinished interior shelves. Paper label, excellent condition, 58" x 42" x 14". $7,000.00.

Gustav Stickley double-door bookcase, with gallery top, eight glass panes in each door, and top and base keyed through the sides. Restored and enhanced original finish. Excellent condition, 56⅓" x 51" x 13". $5,000.00.

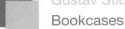

Gustav Stickley double-door bookcase, with gallery top, eight glass panes in each door, V-pulls, and overcoated finish. Paper label, excellent condition, 36" x 48" x 13". $5,500.00.

Gustav Stickley double-door bookcase, with gallery top, three interior shelves, eight glass panes in each door, and hammered-copper V-pulls. The top and bottom are keyed through at the sides. Refinished, paper label, very good condition, 56" x 46" x 13". $4,500.00 – 5,500.00.

Gustav Stickley double-door bookcase, gallery top, eight glass panes in each door, hammered-copper V-pulls, and three interior shelves. The top and base are mortised through the sides. Light overcoated finish, branded "Stickley," very good condition, 56" x 34¾" x 12¾". $3,500.00.

Early Gustav Stickley rare double-door bookcase with mitered mullions, 12 panes per door, gallery top, through-tenons, hammered-copper ring pulls, and excellent original finish. Large red decal, very good condition, 55¾" x 48¾" x 12⅓". $18,500.00 – 22,500.00.

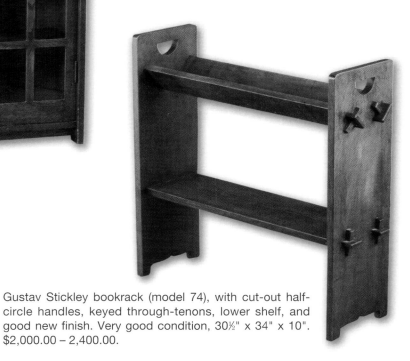

Gustav Stickley bookrack (model 74), with cut-out half-circle handles, keyed through-tenons, lower shelf, and good new finish. Very good condition, 30½" x 34" x 10". $2,000.00 – 2,400.00.

Gustav Stickley spinning book stand, with four partitions, cut-out handle, and original finish. Branded mark, very good condition, 10½" x 12". $1,500.00 – 1,900.00.

Gustav Stickley double-door bookcase, with gallery top, eight glass panes in each door, and through-tenons. Very good condition, 56½" x 47½" x 12½". $3,000.00.

Gustav Stickley double-door bookcase, refinished. Paper label and decal, above average condition, 56" x 43" x 13". $7,500.00. *Photo courtesy of Craftsman Auctions.*

Not Shown

93 Book Cabinet, original finish, 17" x 11" x 40", EX, Eastwood label, $2,500.00.

523 Bookcase, 2 doors, 6 panes per door, 39" x 13" x 45", EX, red decal, signed, $11,000.00.

523 Bookcase, 2 doors, 6 panes per door, iron pulls, 41" x 12" x 44", EX, branded signature, $6,000.00.

525 Bookcase, double doors, keyed tenons, 42" x 12" x 56", VG, $2,600.00.

542 Bookcase, double doors, iron hardware, paneled back, 56" x 36" x 12", VG, $4,250.00.

544 Bookcase, 2 doors, 16 panes per door, board back (rare), 62" x 12" x 56", EX, dated 1901 – 1903, signed, $77,500.00.

700 Bookcase, single door, 3 leaded sections at top, 35" x 14" x 58", EX, paper label, red decal, $12,000.00.

700½ Bookcase, open architectural form w/columns, 3 shelves, 36" x 14" x 58", EX, red decal, signed, $22,000.00.

703 Bookcase, mahogany, double doors, 8 leaded panes per door, 48" x 14" x 58", EX, red decal, $9,000.00.

703½ Bookcase, open, architectural columns, 60" x 14" x 58", EX, Eastwood paper label, $14,000.00.

715 Bookcase, single door, 16 panes, iron hardware , 35" x 13" x 56", EX, paper label, signed, $9,500.00.

715 Bookcase, single door, 16 panes, double-keyed tenons, 39" x 13" x 56", EX, black label, signed, $5,500.00.

716 Bookcase, 28 panes of glass, 36" x 42", EX, $6,000.00.

716 Bookcase, double doors, 8 panes of glass per door, 48" x 56", EX, red decal, $4,750.00.

717 Bookcase, 2 doors, 8 panes per door, copper hardware, 48" x 13" x 56", VG, $5,300.00 – 5,500.00.

717 Bookcase, 28 panes of glass, refinished, 56" x 42", VG, $4,750.00.

718 Bookcase, 2 doors, 8 panes per door, original finish, 54" w, VG, $5,000.00.

718 Bookcase, 2 doors, 8 panes per door, keyed tenon construction, 56" x 47", VG, $6,000.00.

719 Bookcase, 2 doors, 12 panes per door, copper pulls, 54" x 13" x 56", EX, paper label, signed, $9,500.00.

719 Bookcase, 2 doors, 12 panes per door, iron pulls, 60" x 13" x 57", EX, branded, $7,500.00.

Bookcase, open, chamfered back, through-tenon construction, 31" x 12" x 56", VG, red decal, $2,700.00.

Bookcase, 2 doors, 8 panes per door, iron V-pulls, 35" x 13" x 56", VG, branded signature, $4,250.00.

Bookcase, 1904, double doors, copper pulls, 36" x 13" x 56", EX, red decal, signed, $16,000.00.

Bookcase, 2 doors, diamond pattern to mullions, 41" x 64" x 24", EX, paper label, branded mark, $4,500.00.

Not Shown

Bookcase, double glass doors over double wooden cabinet doors, 42" x 14" x 64", EX, red decal, $19,000.00.

Bookcase, early, 56" x 46" x 12", AVG, early box, signed, $3,000.00 – 4,000.00.

Bookcase, 3 doors, 12 panes of glass per door, 73" x 12" x 56", EX, $17,000.00.

Desks

Gustav Stickley rare postcard desk, with overhanging rectangular top, and full gallery with two small cabinet doors and open slots over two drawers. Refinished, red decal, good condition, 40½" x 43" x 25½". $4,000.00.

Early Gustav Stickley fall-front desk, circa 1903, with gallery top, fitted interior, hammered-copper strap hinges, two shelves with through-tenons, and original finish. Marked "Als Ik Kan," very good condition, 51⅛" x 25¾" x 10¾". $6,500.00.

Gustav Stickley rare postcard desk, with full gallery top, two paneled doors, dovetailed corners, two drawers with hammered-copper pulls, good new finish, and red decal. Good condition, 40" x 41½" x 26". $2,300.00.

Gustav Stickley chalet desk, 1902 – 1903, with gallery top, paneled drop-front door, chamfered back, keyed through-tenons, shoe feet, original finish, and red decal. Very good condition, 45¾" x 24". $3,500.00.

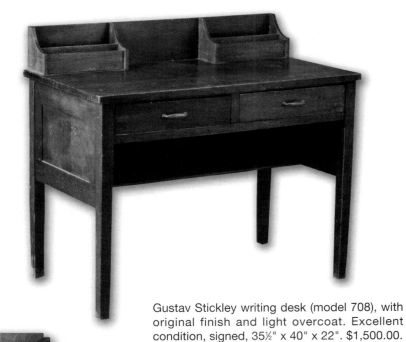

Gustav Stickley writing desk (model 708), with original finish and light overcoat. Excellent condition, signed, 35½" x 40" x 22". $1,500.00.

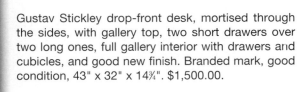

Gustav Stickley drop-front desk, mortised through the sides, with gallery top, two short drawers over two long ones, full gallery interior with drawers and cubicles, and good new finish. Branded mark, good condition, 43" x 32" x 14¾". $1,500.00.

Gustav Stickley drop-front desk (model 729), with gallery top, full gallery interior, two short drawers over three wide ones, hammered-copper drop pulls, and fine new finish. Excellent condition, 45" x 36½" x 15". $3,250.00.

Gustav Stickley rare, roll-top desk (model 619), with interior gallery, locking center drawer, and five additional drawers with iron oval pulls on tapering posts. Refinished, paper label, excellent condition, 46" x 48" x 32". $7,500.00 – 8,000.00.

Gustav Stickley drop-front desk (model 732), with gallery top, full gallery interior, two small drawers over two large ones, wrought iron V-pulls, and original finish. Paper Craftsman label and red decal, good condition, 43" x 32" x 14½". $2,800.00.

Gustav Stickley rare keyhole desk, with leather top, center drawer, recessed shelf, two drawers to each side, hammered-copper oval pulls, original finish, and stamped mark. Good condition, 31" x 50" x 28". $2,900.00.

Gustav Stickley drop-front desk, with original finish and signed. Excellent condition, 44½" x 36½" x 14¾". $3,220.00.
Photo courtesy of Craftsman Auctions.

Early Gustav Stickley slant-front desk, with gallery top, two short drawers over one long, two cabinet doors, strap hinges and hardware, repatinated hardware, and red decal. Very good condition, refinished, 48" x 33" x 14". $3,750.00.

Gustav Stickley rare mahogany drop-front desk, with gallery top, interior fittings, two cabinet doors below, and hammered-copper strap hinges and V-pulls. Refinished, red decal. Excellent condition, 51" x 25" x 31". $5,000.00 – 7,000.00.

Early Gustav Stickley drop-front desk, with gallery top, paneled door and sides, two lower shelves, key lock, strap iron hardware, and large decal. Good condition, 52" x 26" x 11". $2,900.00.

Gustav Stickley rare inlaid drop-front desk, designed by Harvey Ellis. Excellent condition. $8,050.00. *Photo courtesy of Craftsman Auctions.*

Gustav Stickley ladies' desk (model 706), with fine/excellent finish. Branded, excellent condition, 44" x 30" x 11½". $4,427.00. *Photo courtesy of Craftsman Auctions.*

Gustav Stickley postcard desk, with gallery top, two drawers, tapered legs, and excellent original finish. Excellent condition, 38" x 38" x 22". $1,000.00.

Gustav Stickley double-pedestal desk, with two banks of drawers on top, two pull-out shelves and six drawers below, hammered-copper drop pulls, restored original finish to base, refinished top, and red decal. Very good condition, 36½" x 60" x 32". $6,000.00 – 7,000.00.

Gustav Stickley double-pedestal desk, with paneled case, nine drawers with faceted wooden pulls, and lower shelf keyed through the sides. Refinished tenons added, fair condition, 30" x 53½" x 30". $2,000.00.

Gustav Stickley postcard desk, with two letter holders, single drawer with circular wooden pulls, tapered legs, original finish, and branded mark. Fair condition, 35" x 28" x 18". $1,500.00 – 2,000.00.

Gustav Stickley drop-front desk, designed by Harvey Ellis, with overhanging beveled top, paneled door, hammered-copper hinges, gallery interior, lower shelf, original finish, and mid-period red decal. Good condition, 43¾" x 30½" x 11¼". $3,750.00.

Gustav Stickley postcard desk, with gallery top, two small drawers, letter and paper slots, two lower drawers with hammered-iron drop pulls, original finish with overcoat, and red decal. Good condition, 37" x 38" x 23". $1,400.00.

Gustav Stickley writing desk (model 453), with original finish. Good condition, 35½" x 39½" x 22". $1,600.00 – 2,000.00. *Photo courtesy of Craftsman Auctions.*

Gustav Stickley postcard desk, with paneled back and sides, two drawers with replaced brass pulls, recessed lower shelf with keyed through-tenons, and added pencil holder. Good condition, 34¼" x 34" x 20". $1,500.00.

Not Shown

453 Desk, flat top, letter rack, 2 drawers, iron handles, 40" x 22" x 36", G, red decal, $2,100.00.

459 Desk (writing), 28½" x 43" x 24½", G, early decal, $1,495.00.

505 Desk (chalet), paneled door, keyed tenon construction, 20" x 10" x 46", VG, red decal, $2,000.00.

505 Desk (chalet), leather writing pad, 24" x 16" x 46", EX, red decal, $1,800.00.

518 Desk, early, fall-front design, iron strap hardware, 26" x 11" x 52", VG, decal, $6,500.00.

550 Desk, slant front over 3 drawers & 2 doors, 48" x 33", EX, $10,000.00.

708 Desk, desk organizer at top, 2 drawers, lower shelf, 30" x 40" x 22", G, large red decal, $1,100.00 – 1,500.00.

708 Desk (postcard), 2 drawers, 36" x 40" x 22", G, $1,725.00.

708 Desk, 2 drawers, iron pulls, letter rack, lower shelf, 40" x 22" x 36", EX, red decal, paper label, $2,000.00.

709 Desk (table), 28½" x 42" x 24", G, $1,677.00.

709 Desk, leather top, 29" x 42" x 24", AVG, signed, $2,300.00.

710 Desk, 2 drawers on each side of center drawer, copper pulls, 48" x 29" x 30", VG, red decal, $1,500.00.

711 Desk, flat top, center drawer, pull-out writing surfaces, 60" x 31" x 30", G, $1,800.00.

720 Desk, pigeonhole organizer, 2 drawers, 37" x 38", VG, $1,250.00.

720 Desk (writing), 2 drawers, iron pulls, 7 pigeonholes, 38" x 22" x 38", VG, red decal, $2,300.00.

721 Desk, half moon cutouts at top, letter rack, drop-leaf writing surface, 38" w, EX, $425.00 – 500.00.

728 Desk, fall front, single drawer, iron hardware, lower shelf, 30" x 14" x 39", VG, $1,000.00.

729 Desk, fall front, 2 short drawers above 3 long, 36½" x 15" x 43", VG, paper label, branded signature, $2,750.00.

731 Desk, slant front, 2 half drawers over 1 full, 32" x 16" x 44", VG, branded signature, $950.00.

Desk (chalet), 1902, paneled door, wooden lock, 22" x 16" x 46", VG, red decal, $2,000.00.

Desk (keyhole), 4 drawers, 22½" x 42" x 24", FR, $200.00 – 300.00.

Desk (writing armchair), 3 vertical slats under V-back, 28" x 25" x 45", VG, red decal, signed, $900.00.

Desk, posts through top 2 drawers, 30" x 36" x 24", G, $1,100.00.

Desk, leather top, iron hardware, original finish, 34" x 20" x 34", EX, red decal, $4,750.00.

Desk, letter rail over 2 drawers, lower shelf, 34" x 20" x 35", VG, $1,700.00.

Desk (writing), single drawer, iron hardware, 36" x 24" x 29", VG, $1,600.00.

Not Shown

Desk, chestnut, drop front, 3 drawers, 38" x 14" x 48", VG, red decal, $3,500.00.

Desk, oak veneer, drop front, 2 half drawers over 1 full, 43" x 32" x 14", G, $900.00.

Desk, rare, 4 drawers, wooden pulls, 47¼" x 36" x 22", FR, red decal, $7,500.00 – 10,000.00.

Desk (table), overhanging top, tapered legs, 48" x 30" x 29", VG, large early red decal, $2,400.00.

Desk, original finish, 53" x 30" x 29", VG, red decal, signed, $4,250.00.

Desk Set (9 pieces): hammered-copper pad, letter opener, tray, inkwell, calendar, letter rack (8" x 5½"), blotter (25" x 15"), stamp box, and paper clip. Rare set, EX, impressed mark, signed. $4,750.00.

Desk, center drawer, four drawers on each side with wooden faceted pulls, chamfered sides, 54" x 30" x 30", VG, $4,250.00.

361 Office Chair, open under arms, leather seat, 28" x 20" x 37", VG, paper label, $3,500.00.

Gustav Stickley library table, with two drawers, wrought iron hardware, long corbels, and broad lower shelf mortised through stretchers. Refinished, red decal, very good condition, 30" x 54" x 31½". $2,100.00.

Gustav Stickley rare library table, with three drawers, spindled sides, broad lower shelf, hammered-copper pulls, and original finish on base. Top refinished, red decal, good condition, 29" x 54" x 31". $6,000.00.

Gustav Stickley library table (model 619), with three drawers, square posts, broad lower shelf, oval iron pulls, riveted backplates, and original finish to base. Top refinished, large paper label, excellent condition, 30" x 66" x 36". $4,000.00.

Gustav Stickley trestle library table, double-keyed through the legs, with broad lower shelf, original finish to base, and refinished top. Marked, excellent condition, 30" x 48" x 29½". $1,500.00 – 2,000.00.

Gustav Stickley trestle library table, double-keyed through the legs, with rectangular top, lower shelf, excellent original finish to base, and red decal. Excellent condition, 48" x 29" x 28". $1,250.00 – 1,750.00.

Gustav Stickley library table, with two drawers, overhanging rectangular top, hammered-copper hardware, long corbels, lower shelf mortised through side stretchers, original finish to base, and refinished top. Branded "Stickley," very good condition, 30" x 42" x 23¾". $3,750.00.

Gustav Stickley library table, with three drawers, oval iron pulls, broad lower shelf, and original finish. Paper label and red decal, excellent condition, 29" x 66" x 36". $5,000.00.

Gustav Stickley small library table, with overhanging top, blind drawer, one shelf, good original finish, and red decal. Very good condition, 30" x 30" x 20". $2,000.00.

Gustav Stickley library table (model 624), with three drawers with hammered-copper pulls, three vertical slats on each side, one shelf, good original finish, and branded mark. Very good condition, 30" x 54" x 32". $4,500.00.

Gustav Stickley library table, with two draw-ers, oval iron pulls, long corbels, broad lower shelf mortised through stretchers, and original finish. Paper label and red decal, good condition, 30" x 42" x 29½". $1,600.00.

Gustav Stickley single-drawer library table (model 652), with iron V-pulls, overhanging top, one shelf, original finish on base, refinished top, and red decal. Good condition, 29" x 36" x 24". $2,100.00.

Gustav Stickley trestle library table, with original tacked-on leather top, double-keyed through-tenon lower shelf, and red decal. Very good condition, 29" x 48" x 30". $3,000.00.

Not Shown

404 Library Table, vertical keyed tenons, lower shelf, 48" x 30" x 29", VG, $2,000.00.

410-L Library Table, hexagonal leather-covered top, 29½" x 48", EX, $10,000.00.

432 Library Table, early, 2 drawers, V-rail, chamfered knobs, 36" x 24" x 30", VG, numbered, $4,250.00.

456 Library Table, 1902, 2 hidden drawers over lower shelf, 36" x 24" x 29", VG, signed, $3,250.00.

460-L Library Table, 3 drawers, corbeled legs, 66" x 35" x 30", EX, red decal, $15,000.00.

613 Library Table, hammered pulls, 36" x 30", VG, $1,600.00.

614 Library Table, 2 drawers, copper pulls, long corbels, 42" x 29" x 30", VG, $2,900.00.

615 Library Table, 30" x 48" x 29½", EX, signed, $2,900.00.

616 Library Table, 2 drawers, iron oval pulls, 54" x 32" x 30", VG, red decal, $5,500.00.

637 Library Table, 28½" x 48" x 30", G, $1,207.00.

638 Library Table, drop leaf, gate leg, cut corners, 30" x 40" x 42", VG, $950.00.

650 Library Table, single drawer, iron V-pulls, 36" x 24" x 30", VG, red decal, $1,100.00.

651 Library Table, double-keyed stretchers, 48" x 30" x 29", VG, red decal, $1,200.00.

652 Library Table, single drawer, overhanging top, 36" x 24" x 29", G, red decal, signed, $900.00.

653 Library Table, single drawer, lower shelf, 42" x 29", EX, red decal, $1,500.00.

653 Library Table, original finish, 48" x 30" x 29", VG, red decal, $2,700.00.

655 Library Table, rectangular top, 13 vertical spindles, 36" x 24" x 29", VG, paper label, $3,500.00.

657 Library Table, mahogany, 12 spindles to each side, 48" x 30" x 29", VG, red decal, $2,700.00.

659 Library Table, 13 spindles to each side, 54" x 32" x 39", EX, Craftsman label, $8,000.00.

711 Library Table, 30" x 60" x 32", AVG, $5,000.00.

3403 Library Table, trestle form, double-keyed tenons, 36" x 24" x 28", VG, $2,500.00.

Library Table, 2 hidden drawers, low shelf, 29" x 36" x 24", VG, $7,500.00.

Library Table, early, rare, 30½" x 49½" x 29¾", G, large decal, $805.00.

Library Table, overhanging rectangular top, 2 drawers, 30¼" x 35¾" x 23¾", G, red decal, $1,600.00.

Library Table (partners' desk), double top over 4 drawers, 30¾" x 72" x 34½", G, $2,000.00.

Library Table, 3 drawers, 30" x 77½" x 36", AVG, branded signature, $7,500.00.

Not Shown

Library Table, rectangular top over single drawer, 36" x 24" x 25", VG, $1,600.00.

Library Table (desk), single drawer, 48" x 30" x 29", VG, red decal, $2,400.00.

Library Table, 3 drawers, oval iron pulls, 54" x 32" x 30", VG, paper label, $2,500.00.

Library Table, leather top, 2 drawers, 66" x 36" x 30", VG, $5,500.00.

Sewing Rockers & Stands

Gustav Stickley sewing rocker, with three horizontal slats and seat recovered in mustard vinyl. Branded "Stickley," good condition, 32" x 16" x 25". $200.00.

Gustav Stickley maple veneer drop-leaf sewing stand, designed by Harvey Ellis, with copper and fruitwood inlay to leaves and to three drawer fronts, and with circular pulls, tapered legs, and red decal. Excellent condition, 28" x 18" x 16". $5,500.00.

Gustav Stickley spindled-back sewing rocker with tacked-on new leather seat, overcoated original finish, and paper label. Good condition, 32½" x 18" x 24". $550.00.

Not Shown

303 Sewing Rocker, rope support, leather cushion, 17" x 16" x 33", EX, red decal, $275.00.

337 Sewing Rocker, original finish, 33½" x 16¾" x 16¼", AVG+, branded paper label, $350.00.

359 Sewing Rocker, 9 spindles to back, 26" x 21" x 37", EX, red decal, $750.00.

373 Sewing Rocker, 9 spindles to back, 5 spindles to sides, 16" x 24" x 36", VG, $325.00.

387 Sewing Rocker, 3 vertical slats to back, 3 under seat, 20" x 18" x 43", EX, red decal, signed, $850.00 – 1,000.00.

630 Sewing Rocker, 2 drawers, copper ring pulls, 19" x 18" x 28", VG, $1,300.00.

2635 Sewing Rocker, 2 horizontal slats to back, 18" x 25" x 31", EX, red decal, signed, $800.00.

Sewing Rocker, 3 horizontal slats to back, leather seat, 17" x 26" x 32", EX, red decal, $250.00.

630 Sewing Table, 3 drawers, wooden knobs, two 2" drop leaves, 17" x 17" x 28", VG, red decal, paper label, $2,000.00.

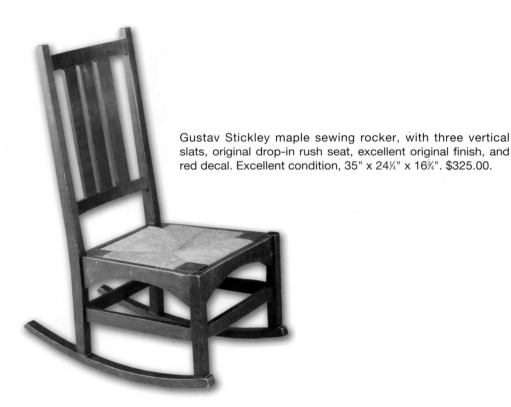

Gustav Stickley maple sewing rocker, with three vertical slats, original drop-in rush seat, excellent original finish, and red decal. Excellent condition, 35" x 24¼" x 16¾". $325.00.

Gustav Stickley Tree of Life magazine stand, with square overhanging top, flaring side panels with tree motif, four shelves, and original finish. Good condition, 43½" x 12½". $1,700.00.

Gustav Stickley magazine stand, designed by Harvey Ellis, with overhanging rectangular top, arched aprons, three shelves, arched sides, and original finish. Excellent condition, 41¾" x 21½" x 12". $2,300.00.

Gustav Stickley magazine stand, with D-shaped handles, four shelves, arched base, original finish, and red decal. Excellent condition, 39¾" x 13¾" x 10". $1,900.00.

Gustav Stickley magazine stand, with beveled top, paneled sides, three shelves, original finish, and red box decal. Excellent condition, 34¾" x 15½" x 15½". $3,250.00.

Gustav Stickley magazine stand, designed by Harvey Ellis, with overhanging top, arched apron, three shelves, and red decal. Good condition, 41¾" x 21½" x 13". $2,900.00.

Gustav Stickley magazine stand, with beveled overhanging top, three open shelves, and good new finish. Very good condition, 53¼" x 15¼" x 15¼". $2,000.00.

Gustav Stickley magazine stand (model 72), with waxed original finish in above average condition. Signed, very good condition, 42" x 22" x 13". $2,500.00. *Photo courtesy of Craftsman Auctions.*

Not Shown

72 Magazine Stand, 3 shelves, rectangular top, 29" x 23" x 49", VG, $2,900.00.

79 Magazine Stand, cut-out handles, 40" x 14" x 10", G, signed, $2,472.00.

506 Magazine Stand, beveled top, 4 shelves, refinished, 39" x 16", VG, $4,000.00.

514 Magazine Stand, 3 shelves, original condition, 15" x 14" x 35", EX, red decal, $3,000.00.

514 Magazine Stand, paneled sides, 4 shelves, 16" x 15" x 45", EX, red decal, $3,000.00.

547 Magazine Stand, 3 shelves, 15" x 15" x 35", EX, red box, $4,500.00.

548 Magazine Stand, early, beveled top, 15" x 44", VG, $2,600.00.

548 Magazine Stand, 4 shelves, paneled sides, 16" x 16" x 16", VG, $2,600.00.

1902 Magazine Stand, 1902, 3 shelves, 15" x 15" x 35", VG, red decal, $9,000.00.

Magazine Stand, Tree of Life design, 4 shelves, 13" x 43", EX, $2,200.00.

Magazine Stand, 3 shelves, single slat to side, 16" x 13" x 31", VG, red decal, $1,100.00.

Magazine Stand, 4 shelves, cut-out sides, 20" x 15" x 36", VG, red decal, $1,400.00.

Magazine Stand, 3 shelves, single wide slat to side, 27" x 12" x 30", VG, branded signature, $1,200.00.

Magazine Stand, 33" x 19" x 14", G, $1,035.00.

Magazine Stand, 3 shelves, paneled sides, 35" x 15¼" x 15¼", G, $2,000.00.

Magazine Stand, 3 shelves, arched sides, 41¾" x 27½" x 13", G, $2,300.00.

Not Shown

11 Plant Stand (yeddo stand), Grueby tile, 24" x 15" x 5", EX, paper shop tag, $6,000.00.

41 Plant Stand, splayed legs, 14" x 14" x 28", EX, red decal, $1,300.00.

604 Plant Stand, 26" x 20", G, $1,300.00.

660 Plant Stand, square top, cut corners, 18" x 18" x 20", VG, paper label, branded signature, $2,100.00.

704 Plant Stand, rectangular top, turned legs, 22" x 18" x 18", VG, $1,200.00.

Plant Stand, clipped corners, 22" x 17" x 17", G, paper label, $3,500.00.

Gustav Stickley plant stand, with rail, arched apron, arched stretchers, good new finish. Excellent condition, 30" x 12½" x 12¾". $2,000.00.

Early Gustav Stickley plant stand, with square top, arched apron, H-shaped keyed through-stretcher, and 1902 decal. Refinished, very good condition, 25½" x 14". $1,800.00.

Gustav Stickley tabouret, with circular top and cloud-lift cross stretchers, overcoated base, and red decal. Refinished, good condition, 18¼" x 16". $700.00.

Gustav Stickley tabouret, with circular top, arched cross stretchers, and new finish. Very good condition, 16" x 14". $600.00.

Early Gustav Stickley early mahogany lotos tabouret, with pentagonal top, five cut-out legs and star shaped stretchers below, overcoated original finish, and early paper label. Very good condition, 20" x 19". $2,400.00.

Not Shown

601 Tabouret, refinished, 16" x 14", FR, $500.00 – 700.00.

602 Tabouret, 16" dia., VG, red decal, $900.00.

603 Tabouret, 20" x 18", VG, $800.00 – 1,200.00.

Tabouret, circular top, cloud-lift cross stretchers, 17¾" x 16", G, $600.00.

Tabouret, square tile, flush tenons, 17" x 17" x 22", EX, dated 1901 – 1903, red decal, signed, $80,000.00.

Tabouret, circular top, arched cross-stretcher, 18" x 20", VG, $1,100.00.

Tabouret, refinished, 20" x 18", VG, $977.00.

Tabouret, square top, lower shelf, 25½" x 18", G, paper label, $425.00.

Tabouret, circular top, refinished 26" x 20", VG, $500.00 – 700.00.

Tabouret, circular top, 19¾" x 18", G, $650.00.

Tabouret, early, through-tenons, original finish, VG, early box, $800.00 – 1,000.00.

Early Gustav Stickley celandine circular tea table (model 27), with top carved and incised with a celandine poppy motif, cut-out cross stretchers, carved and keyed through floriform legs (a very rare design marking the transition from the Art Nouveau to the Arts and Crafts aesthetic), mint finish, and paper label. Good condition, 24" x 20". $10,000.00.

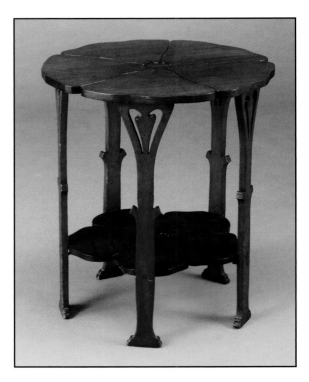

Gustav Stickley poppy mahogany side table, with carved top and lower shelf, reticulated legs, original finish to base, refinished top, and paper label. Good condition, 23¾" x 19½". $3,750.00.

Early Gustav Stickley lamp table, with flush circular top, corseted cross-stretchers mortised through the legs and topped by a finial, original finish, and 1902 – 1903 decal. Excellent condition, Size: 28" x 23½". $5,000.00.

Gustav Stickley lamp table, with clip-corner top, lower shelf, arched cross-stretchers mortised through the legs, original finish, and Craftsman paper label. Excellent condition, 29" x 24". $1,900.00.

Gustav Stickley lamp table (model 644), with circular top, arched cross-stretchers mortised through the legs, original finish, Eastwood paper label, and red decal. Excellent condition, 29" x 30". $1,700.00.

Gustav Stickley director's table, with rectangular overhanging top, pegged trestle base with broad apron, and paper label. Refinished, excellent condition, 29½" x 84" x 42". $9,500.00.

Gustav Stickley nightstand, with two drawers, back-splash, overhanging top, circular wooden pulls, tapered legs, and good original finish to base. Marked, very good condition, 30¼" x 20" x 18". $1,900.00.

Gustav Stickley lamp table (model 644), with mortised legs, circular top, and arched cross-stretchers. Topped by a finial, marked "Als Ik Kan," very good condition, 28¾" x 29½". $2,000.00.

Gustav Stickley rare hexagonal table, with original tacked-on leather top, stacked arched stretchers keyed through the legs and topped by a finial, and fine original medium brown finish and leather. Excellent condition, 30" x 55". $20,000.00.

Gustav Stickley occasional table, with circular overhanging top, faceted finial over arched cross-stretchers, very good original finish, and red decal. Excellent condition, 29" x 24". $1,900.00.

Early Gustav Stickley drink stand, from 1901, with square top, cloud-lift apron, center stretcher keyed through trumpet side stretchers, fine original finish, and paper label. 22½" x 14". $2,000.00 – 3,000.00.

Gustav Stickley rare table, with circular top, keyhole apron, turned and flared legs, and good original finish. Good condition, 24½" x 24". $1,500.00.

Gustav Stickley director's table (model 631), with overhanging rectangular top, trestle base, pegged construction, and good new finish. Excellent condition, 29¼" x 96" x 48¼". $10,000.00.

Not Shown

436 Stand, circular top, 24" x 28", VG, red decal, $3,750.00.

605 Stand (telephone), square top over lower shelf, 14" x 14" x 30", VG, branded signature, $15,000.00.

605 Stand (telephone), 29¼" x 14", G, $850.00.

642 Stand, backsplash, 2 small drawers, 22" x 16" x 29", VG, signed, $1,600.00.

641 Stand, 2 drawers, square top, 20" x 31", VG, red decal, $1,300.00.

   Stand (telephone), open shelf under top, 21" x 14" x 30", VG, paper label, $1,800.00.

   Stand, pedestal, narrow circular top, 36" x 4¼" x 17", VG, $2,200.00.

   Stand, round, 25" x 24", G, $575.00.

   Stand (drink), copper top, 28" x 18", VG, signed, $2,587.00.

53-T Table, cut corners, square top, Grueby tile, 17" x 22", EX, paper label, branded signature, $11,000.00.

407 Table, leather top, splayed legs, cross-stretcher base, 48" x 30", VG, $2,800.00.

419 Table (chess), leather top, keyed tenons, 39" x 27" x 27", EX , $10,000.00.

424 Table (lunch), rectangular top, 41" x 28" x 28", VG, large red decal, signed, $1,600.00.

439 Table, through-tenon stretcher construction, 26" x 26", EX, red box mark, signed, $4,500.00.

440 Table, thick top, through-tenons on top & bottom, 30" x 28", VG, $2,700.00 – 3,000.00.

441 Table, through-tenons, stacked stretchers, 36" x 30", VG, red decal, $2,400.00.

604 Table (tea), arched stretcher, 26" x 20", VG, paper label, $2,900.00.

604 Table (tea), circular top, 26" x 26", G, $950.00.

605 Table (tea), round top, cross-stretchers, EX, red decal, $1,900.00.

607 Table, circular top, round lower shelf, 24" x 21", EX, red decal, $3,500.00.

608 Table (tea), 26" x 24", VG, branded, signed, $1,500.00.

609 Table (center), arched stretchers, 36" x 30", VG, red decal, $1,500.00.

611 Table, cut-corner top, lower shelf, 24" x 29", EX, red decal, paper label, $3,750.00.

627 Table, round table, original finish, arched stretchers, 48" x 30", VG, red decal, $1,600.00 – 2,400.00.

627 Table (trestle), rectangular top, 29¼" x 96" x 48¼", EX, $10,000.00.

631 Table (director's), large rectangular top, 86" x 47" x 29", VG, red decal, $14,000.00.

631 Table (director's), 96" x 48" x 30", EX, large red decal, $14,000.00.

Stickley Brothers
Furniture Company
(1892 – 1954)

The Stickley Brothers Furniture Company was founded by Albert and John Stickley in 1892. The company was located first in Binghampton, New York, and then in Grand Rapids, Michigan. Albert and John made the move to Michigan, leaving Charles in Binghampton, where he and an uncle continued the operation under a different name. After several years, John left the company in Michigan to rejoin his brother Leopold in New York. (Later, these two brothers formed their own furniture company, the L. & J. G. Stickley Furniture Company, mentioned in chapter III of this guide.) Albert and John sold furniture under the Quaint label; *quaint* was the British name for Arts & Crafts furniture. The brothers also operated a plant in London between 1897 and 1902, to assemble and finish furniture for the British market. Their lower quality lines used veneers to imitate quartersawn oak, and pulls on their furniture were stamped of brass instead of copper. Iron dowels were used as through-tenons, and plywood was used for drawer bottoms instead of solid wood. Stickley Brothers furniture can be found today with a paper label that reads "made by Stickley Brothers, Grand Rapids, Michigan," or sometimes found with a brass plate or decal with the words "Quaint Furniture." Furniture produced by Stickley Brothers had very fine inlay and decorative cutouts. Stickley Brothers produced furniture in not only the Arts and Crafts style, but in Colonial Revival style as well. The company also produced metal accessories and copper items as well as the very popular furniture line very much sought after today. This line includes desks, bookcases, armchairs, china cabinets, rockers, sideboards, and other furniture and accessories that are listed throughout this chapter of the price guide.

275½ Armchair, 5 vertical slats to back, open under arms, 26" x 21" x 38", VG, numbered 275½, $700.00.

352½ Armchair, 4 vertical slats to back, open under arms, 25" x 21" x 38", VG, Quaint metal tag, $150.00.

375½ Armchair, refinished, 39" x 26" x 21", G, $345.00.

728½ Armchair, 6 vertical stats to back, 28" x 26" x 41", VG, numbered, branded, $750.00.

873½ Armchair, 3 vertical slats to back, 26" x 23" x 36", EX, Quaint tag, $450.00.

887½ Armchair, 5 vertical slats to back, 27" x 22" x 35", VG, $350.00.

891½ Armchair, 4 vertical slats to back, drop-in seat, 27" x 22" x 35", VG, $600.00.

917½ Armchair, posts through front & back, 31" x 21" x 36", VG, paper label, $400.00.

Armchair, 3 tapered slats, 25" x 22" x 34", EX, $750.00.

Armchair, 6 slats under each arm, 6 vertical slats to back, 27" x 24" x 40", VG, $400.00.

Armchair, 8 spindles to back, 27" x 27" x 43", EX, Quaint tag, $950.00.

Armchair, refinished, 29" x 22" x 42", VG, $450.00.

Armchair, winged back, 5 slats to back, 3 slats under arms, 30" x 30" x 38", EX, Quaint tag, $325.00.

Armchair, vertical slats to back and under arms, 37" x 27" x 33", G, Quaint tag, $350.00.

Armchair, plank seat, vertical slats, 38" x 27" x 22", G, $300.00.

Armchairs (pair), horizontal slats, 39" x 25" x 19", FR, $600.00.

Armchair, ladder-back, open arms, 41" x 27" x 25", VG, paper label, $550.00.

Armchair, 4 vertical backslats, open arms, 43½"x 27½" x 23½", G, $300.00.

Armchair, 4 backslats, spring seat, 48", G, $375.00.

Stickley Brothers daybed, with sloping side panels, head-board and footboard mortised through tapered legs, original finish, and metal tag. Stenciled "235-401," good condition, 25½" x 29¼" x 76½". $1,500.00 – 2,000.00.

Double bed, with headboard with panels and narrow vertical slats, tapered feet, side rails, and good original finish. Stenciled "9001½," very good condition, 40" x 56½" x 80½". $1,500.00 – 2,000.00.

Stickley Brothers double-door bookcase, with gallery top, doors with faux mullions and divided by a marquetry panel depicting a peach tree, and very good original finish. Stenciled "5080," very good condition, 55" x 49¾" x 13¼". $6,000.00 – 8,000.00.

Stickley Brothers double-door bookcase, with slotted gallery top, single panes, excellent original finish, and brass tag. 50" x 35½" x 12". $3,250.00.

Stickley Brothers double-door bookcase, with paneled sides, eight panes and faux-mullioned lattice to each door, and original finish. Overcoated to top only, Quaint metal tag, good conditon, 53" x 48" x 12½". $2,900.00.

Stickley Brothers bookrack, with gallery top, three spindles to each side, four shelves, and original finish. Good condition, 39" x 26½" x 13". $1,100.00.

Stickley Brothers triple-door bookcase, with original dark finish. Excellent condition, 53½" x 59" x 12". $5,175.00.
Photo courtesy of Craftsman Auctions.

Not Shown

4762 Bookcase, 2 doors, 8 panes per door, 36" x 12" x 46", VG, numbered, $2,300.00.

4770 Bookcase, 2 doors, 8 panes per door, 36" x 13" x 52", VG, numbered, $1,900.00.

4776 Bookcase, 3 doors, 8 panes per door, 3 shelves, 62" x 12" x 47", VG, $3,500.00.

Bookcase, 2 doors, 2 panes at top, 36" x 13" x 56", VG, $2,100.00.

Bookcase, 2 door, 48" x 12" x 48", EX, Quaint metal tag, $1,200.00.

Bookcase, rare, 2 doors, paneled slats, 49" x 55" x 13", VG, $7,000.00.

Bookcase, 2 doors, 55" x 49" x 12", EX, paper label, $3,277.00.

Bookcase, 3 doors with leaded glass squares, 60" x 59", EX, $4,750.00.

Chairs

Not Shown

479½ Chair, 3 vertical slats under arched rail, 18" x 16" x 37", VG, Quaint metal tag, $200.00.

559½ Chair, bow arm, high back, horizontal seat, 27" x 22" x 44", VG, Quaint tag, $1,000.00.

84½ Chairs (cafe, set of 4), heart-shaped cutouts to backslat, 28¾" x 16½" x 15", VG, Quaint decal, $1,200.00.

Chair (wing), 5 vertical side slats, 44" x 34" x 32", G, $650.00.

Children's Furniture

Not Shown

4211½ Highchair (baby), 19" x 19" x 40", VG, Quaint metal tag, $1,000.00.

Rocker (Morris), 30" x 21" x 23", VG, $1,500.00.

Chests of Drawers

Not Shown

9011 Chest, 2 drawers over 3, copper hardware, 42" x 20" x 47", EX, numbered, $2,400.00.

9022 Chest, 4 small drawers, 4 long copper pulls, 36" x 18" x 56", VG, numbered, $3,000.00.

Stickley Brothers chest of drawers, with two small drawers over four large, backsplash, arched toeboard, square brass pulls, and brass tag. Refinished, very good condition, 40" x 38" x 21". $2,500.00.

Stickley Brothers chest (model 9036), with six drawers, arched backsplash, inset panel sides, circular wooden pulls, cleaned original finish, replaced knob, Quaint metal tag, and stenciled number. Good condition, 33½" x 33" x 20". $1,500.00.

Stickley Brothers chest of drawers, with pivoting mirror, two small drawers over four large, circular wooden pulls, original finish, and Quaint metal tag. Very good condition, 7½" x 36" x 21". $1,900.00 – 2,000.00.

8644 China Cabinet, 68" x 48" x 17½", EX, $4,000.00.

8842 China Cabinet, 2 doors, 58" x 15" x 62", VG, $1,900.00.

China Cabinet, 2 doors, original finish, 62" x 42" x 17", F, $2,587.00.

Stickley Brothers double-door china cabinet, with over-hanging rectangular top, tapered posts, glass panel doors, hammered-copper hardward and interior shelves, original finish, replaced glass panel on side, and Quaint label. Good condition, 54½" x 35" x 16". $1,600.00 – 2,000.00.

Stickley Brothers double-door china cabinet (model 2017), with original finish with overcoat. Average condition, 64" x 46" x 17½". $3,000.00.
Photo courtesy of Craftsman Auctions.

Stickley Brothers double-door china cabinet (model 8852), with backsplash, mirrored top in paneled interior, three shelves, single pane doors with hammered-copper hardware, and good original finish. Branded mark and stenciled number, good condition, 59" x 46" x 15¼". $2,000.00.

Costumers

Not Shown

188 Costumer, double posts, shoe base, 69" h, G, $1,200.00.

Costumer, double, 68" x 17½", VG, paper label, signed, $1,380.00.

Costumer, 72" x 14½" x 20", VG, $600.00.

Desks

Stickley Brothers fall-front desk, with gallery top, cut-out and mortised sides, fitted interior, three drawers over one shelf, riveted curvilinear patinated hardware, and original finish. Good condition, 47¼" x 32" x 13". $2,200.00.

Stickley Brothers postcard desk, with letter slots, single drawer with square wooden pulls, and spindled sides. Refinished, split to top, loose, on casters. As-is condition, 35¼" x 36" x 23". $300.00.

Stickley Brothers single-drawer desk, with slatted bookshelf to each side, broad lower shelf, replaced pulls, and Stickley Brothers oval paper label. Good condition, 30" x 44" x 28". $650.00.

Stickley Brothers drop-front desk, with single drawer, ring pulls, key lock, interior gallery, overcoated finish, and paper label. Fair condition, 41" x 29" x 16½". $750.00 – 1,000.00.

Not Shown

171 Desk, 2 drawers, copper pulls, 36" x 24" x 36", VG, $850.00 – 1,100.00.

2802 Desk, mahogany, 3 drawers, 42" x 28" x 30", VG, Quaint metal tag, $300.00.

6178 Desk, slotted organizer, single drawer, 34" x 22" x 34", VG, $1,600.00.

6516 Desk, slant front over drawer, shoe base, 47" x 30", VG, $1,900.00.

Desk, slatted sides, shelves, drawers, 28½" x 40" x 28½", VG, $500.00.

Desk, mahogany, 5 drawers, brass pulls, 30" x 50" x 52", G, $800.00.

Desk, single drawer, letter organizer, 34" x 22" x 34", VG, Quaint metal tag, signed, $1,200.00.

Desk (postcard), 2 small drawers, open cubbies, 35¾" x 36" x 22", VG, branded "Stickley Brothers," Quaint decal, $700.00.

Desk, trapezoidal top, 3 drawers, 36" x 23" x 36", G, $750.00.

Desk (chair), plank seat, 38" x 16" x 15", G, $535.00.

Desk, drop front, original finish, 42" x 28" x 16", G, $460.00 – 475.00.

Desk (kneehole), 3 drawers, 42" x 28" x 30", G, Quaint metal tag, $425.00.

Desk (inlaid writing), 42" x 36" x 26", VG, Quaint metal tag, $1,100.00.

Desk, flat top, gallery on back, 2 drawers each side, 46" x 23" x 36", G, branded signature, $950.00.

Desk, drop front, 46½" x 36" x 16½", G, $600.00.

Stickley Brothers split-pedestal extension dining table (model 2428), with shoe feet, two additional leaves, and Quaint metal tag. Refinished, very good condition, 29½" x 48". $2,400.00.

Stickley Brothers extension dining table, with circular top, three additional leaves, pedestal base with shoe feet, casters, original finish to base, refinished top, and one cracked foot. Missing some plugs, branded mark and paper label, as-is condition, 29" x 54". $2,300.00.

Stickley drawer table, with flush top, three slats to each side, and lower shelf. Good condition, 30" x 24" x 22". $1,250.00 – 1,750.00.

Stickley Brothers pedestal extension dining table, with circular top, five leaves, casters, old refinish, and minor wear to top. Good condition, 30" x 54". $4,500.00.

Stickley Brothers drop-leaf table, with square top, end stretchers, original finish with overcoat, and branded mark. Good condition, 29½" x 30". $1,200.00.

Stickley Brothers dining table, with five leaves. Refinished, paper label, excellent condition, 30" x 54". Good condition. $4,500.00. *Photo courtesy of Craftsman Auctions.*

Set of six Stickley Brothers dining chairs, five side chairs (model 479½) and one armchair (model 479¼), each with three vertical backslats and upholsterd seat cushions. Refinished, very poor condition, 37" x 19" x 18". $2,200.00.

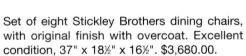

Set of eight Stickley Brothers dining chairs, with original finish with overcoat. Excellent condition, 37" x 18½" x 16½". $3,680.00.

Stickley Brothers side table, with rectangular top, lower shelf, and stretchers mortised through the posts. Good condition, 29½" x 26" x 20". $600.00 – 800.00.

Stickley Brothers side table, with copper-clad circular top, stretchers mortised through flaring legs, and original finish with overcoat. Stenciled "406-2864," good condition, 26" x 25". $2,300.00 – 2,500.00.

Stickley Brothers split-pedestal dining table (model 2870), with shoe feet. Refinished, stenciled "2870," excellent condition, 29" x 54". $2,000.00.

141

Not Shown

379½ Dining Chairs (set of 6), vertical slats under top rail, 18" x 38", EX, branded number, signed, $2,200.00.

479½ Dining Chairs (set of 8), three vertical slats under top rail, 18" x 16" x 37", VG, numbered, $2,900.00.

2422 Dining Table, circular top, flared base, 54" x 30", VG, $2,100.00.

2424 Dining Table, circular top, 48" x 29", G, $1,000.00.

2870 Dining Table, pedestal, shoe feet, 29" x 54", EX, stenciled "2870", $2,000.00.

2640 Dining Table, circular top, square base, 48" x 29", VG, $1,300.00.

2656 Dining Table, circular top, 54" x 30", G, metal tag, $850.00.

2674 Dining Table and 4 Chairs, 35" x 30", VG, $2,100.00.

Dining Table, round oak, 5 legs, G, $1,200.00 – 1,500.00.

Dining Table, 5 legs, 2 leaves, 30" x 48", VG, paper label, $2,500.00.

Dining Table, corbeled pedestal, 30" x 54", EX, $3,500.00.

Dining Table, circular top, shoe feet, 31½" x 48", VG, stenciled, $2,000.00.

Dining Table, thick round top, 44" x 30", VG, $1,500.00.

Dining Table, square base, corbeled feet, 48" x 29", VG, Quaint tag, $2,200.00.

Dining Table, round top, square pedestal, 54" x 30", VG, Quaint tag, $2,000.00.

Dining Table, pedestal base, 60" x 30", EX, paper label, branded, $4,500.00.

2501 Table (side), circular top, 26" x 29", VG, $1,200.00.

2504 Table, circular top, square lower shelf, 24" x 30", VG, numbered, $600.00.

2870 Table (side), copper-clad top, 26" x 25", G, stenciled "406-2864," $2,300.00 – 2,500.00.

2884 Table, tapered legs, 3 spindles to each side, 34" x 17", EX, Quaint tag, signed, $1,200.00.

5671 Table, 3 vertical slats to each side, 15" x 24", G, numbered 5671, $425.00.

Table, drop leaf, original finish, 30" x 12" x 30", EX, $950.00.

Table (side), lower shelf, 3 spindles to each side, 30" x 18" x 30", VG, $950.00.

9032 Dresser, 2 half drawers over 4 full drawers, 38" x 22" x 50", VG, signed, $2,100.00.

Dresser, 3 drawers, wooden knobs, 44" x 22" x 66", VG, Quaint metal tag, $700.00.

Dresser, inlaid mirror, 67" x 45" x 22", VG, $575.00.

Stickley Brothers vanity (model 9035), with paneled sides and back, five drawers with round wooden pulls, triple mirror, original finish, and Quaint decal. Good condition, 55" x 44" x 20". $1,900.00.

Drink Stands & Tables

Not Shown

2615 Drink Table, copper clad, round top, 18" x 28", VG, $950.00.

Drink Stand, square top, 3 slats to each side, 24½" x 15", G, paper label, $1,200.00.

Stickley Brothers copper-topped drink stand, with circular top, flaring legs, arched aprons, excellent original finish, and Quaint metal tag. Excellent condition, 27¾" x 18". $2,600.00.

Footstools

Not Shown

Footstool, 8" x 8½" x 12", G, $250.00.

Not Shown

Hall Chair, solid back w/cutout at top, 15" x 16" x 38", EX, paper label, $900.00.

Hall Chair, floral design on back, 15" x 44", VG, early paper label, $1,000.00.

Hall Chair, tapered back, vertical slats, 38½" x 16" x 14¼", G, $600.00.

Hall Chair, 5-sided back, floral inlay, 40", G, $800.00.

3822 Hall Seat, vertical slats over seat, 42" x 17" x 34", VG, $2,400.00.

Hall Seat, horizontal chamfered boards to back, 42" x 27" x 60", EX, Quaint metal tag, $2,100.00.

2720 Hall Table, single drawer, copper pulls, 36" x 20" x 30", VG, $1,000.00.

Hall Tree, 4 hooks, 17" x 17" x 72", VG, Quaint metal tag, $600.00.

Hall Tree, 84" x 32" x 35", VG, $3,750.00.

Hall Tree, double costumer, iron hooks, VG, $550.00.

Stickley Brothers rare hall seat, with original finish with light overcoat and Quaint metal tag. Good condition, 34" x 48" x 17½". $1,495.00.

Lamps & Lighting

Not Shown

Lamps (table), hammered-copper, 6 panels, mica & copper shade, 15" x 18", EX, $4,000.00.

Lamp, hammered-copper base & shade, cream & brown glass panel, 22" x 20", EX, $2,800.00.

Lamp (table), copper & brass, 3 sockets, umbrella shade, 24" x 22", EX, $2,600.00.

Lamp (table), hammered-copper, 6 kokomo glass panels, 28" x 16", EX, $3,000.00.

Lamp Tables

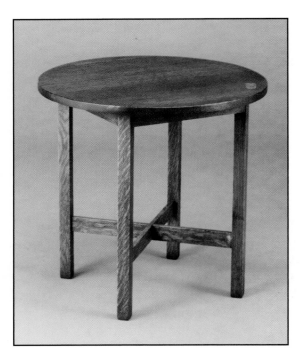

Stickley Brothers lamp table, with circular top, straight cross-stretchers, and apron. Refinished, Quaint tag, very good condition, 23¾" x 23½". $550.00.

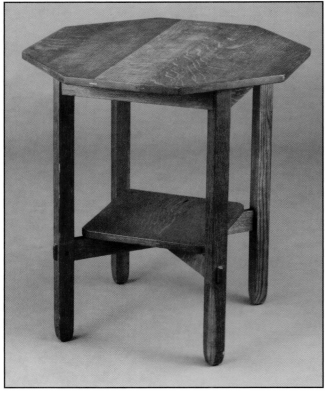

Stickley Brothers lamp table, with octogonal top, square lower shelf, good original finish, and Quaint metal tag. Very good condition, 29½" x 26¼" x 26¼". $1,300.00.

Stickley Brothers lamp table, with rectangular overhanging top, straight apron, mortised lower shelf, tapered legs, and original finish. Good condition, 29½" x 26" x 20". $950.00.

Stickley Brothers lamp table (model 2505), with circular top, original black leather with embossed tacks, square apron, lower shelf, tapered feet, and original finish. Stenciled "6729," paper label, excellent condition, 30" x 26". $2,300.00.

Stickley Brothers lamp table, with circular top covered in tacked-on brown leather, square lower shelf, tapered legs, new finish and leather, and paper label. Very good condition, 30" x 26½". $1,100.00.

Not Shown

2312 Lamp Table, refinished, 30" x 30", VG, Quaint tag, $800.00.

2882 Lamp Table, rectangular top, vertical spindles, 30" x 18" x 30", VG, Quaint metal tag, signed, $1,300.00.

Lamp Table, refinished, 26" x 28", VG, $925.00.

Lamp Table, round, 28½" x 35½", G, $977.00.

Lamp Table, circular shelf, 30¼" x 24½", G, $1,035.00.

Lamp Table, original finish, 30" x 30", VG, $850.00 – 1,000.00.

Lamp Table, circular shelf, 30½" x 26", G, $1,035.00.

Library Tables

Stickley Brothers single-drawer library table, with overhanging top, vertical side slats, lower shelf, Mackmurdo feet, ring pulls, original finish, and minor staining to top. Backplates to pulls missing, as-is condition, 29" x 42" x 28". $1,300.00.

Stickley Brothers double-drawer library table, with ring pulls, long corbels, two side slats, paired stretchers mortised through the sides, very good original finish, minor staining to top, and Quiant furniture mark. Very good condition, 30" x 48" x 30". $2,100.00.

Stickley Brothers library table, with overhanging top, three drawers, riveted and patinated brass hardware, through-tenons, new finish, and paper label. Good condition, 30" x 60½" x 35½". $1,400.00.

Stickley Brothers double-drawer library table, with overhanging top, spindled sides, lower shelf, and original finish. Good condition, 29" x 48" x 30". $950.00 – 1,000.00.

Stickley Brothers library table, with overhanging top, three drawers with brass hardware, cut-out escutcheons, broad lower shelf, and refinished top. 30" x 60" x 36". $1,500.00 – 2,500.00.

Stickley Brothers double-drawer library table (model 2442), with flush rectangular top, hammered-copper drop pulls, plank stretchers mortised through the sides, and original finish. Each drawer numbered 41, very good condition, 30¼" x 54" x 32". $1,900.00.

Stickley Brothers double-drawer library table, with overhanging rectangular top, angular drop pulls, lower shelf, very good original finish, and Quaint metal tag. Very good condition, 34" x 48" x 33¾". $1,000.00 – 1,500.00.

Stickley Brothers single-drawer library table, with overhanging rectangular top, copper ring pulls and backplates, slatted sides, lower shelf, Mackmurdo feet, original finish to base, and refinished top. Very good condition, 29¾" x 48" x 35". $1,500.00.

Stickley Brothers library table, with cut-out slats to sides, two lower drawers with copper ring pulls, some looseness, and remnants of branded number. Refinished, good condition, 28½" x 40¼" x 28¼". $550.00.

Not Shown

253 Library Table, 2 drawers, lower shelf, Mackmurdo feet, 48" x 28" x 29", G, Quaint metal tag, $700.00.

2654 Library Table, 3 slats at side, through-tenons, 48" x 30" x 30", EX, $475.00.

2860 Library Table, 3 drawers, copper hardware, 26" x 29", VG, numbered 2860, $3,250.00.

2896 Library Table, single drawer, 40" x 26" x 30", VG, Quaint tag, $475.00.

Library Table, single drawer, copper pulls, 24" x 22" x 30", EX, $1,500.00.

Library Table, single drawer, rectangular top, 29" x 40" x 26", VG, Quaint metal tag, $950.00.

Library Table, single drawer, square post, 29½" x 42" x 28", G, metal tag, $850.00.

Library Table, leather top, 29½" x 46" x 27", EX, $1,437.00.

Library Table, 2 drawers, rectangular top, slatted sides, Mackmurado feet, 29½" x 46" x 29¾", G, $800.00.

Library Table, slatted sides, cutouts, 30" x 35½" x 32½", G, $575.00.

Library Table, 2 drawers, flush top, 30" x 48" x 27¾", G, stenciled number, $850.00.

Library Table (prairie design), rectangular top, 40" x 26" x 30", VG, Quaint metal tag, signed, $2,400.00.

Library Table, 3 slats at side, through-tenons, 48" x 30" x 30", EX, $475.00.

Library Table, 2 drawers, tapered legs, 52" x 32" x 29", EX, $550.00.

Library Table, mahogany, 54" x 36" x 30", VG, $600.00.

Liquor Cabinets

Not Shown

Liquor Cabinet, pull-out copper tray, 22" x 16" x 36", VG, $2,000.00.

Liquor Cabinet, 4 doors, 51" x 27", G, $2,700.00.

Magazine Stands

Not Shown

4600 Magazine Stand, 3 shelves, 16" x 13" x 31", EX, Quaint metal tag, $950.00.

4602 Magazine Stand, original finish, 16" x 12" x 51", VG, paper label, $700.00.

4602 Magazine Stand, 5 shelves, 2 slats on each side, 16" x 13" x 47", VG, paper label, numbered 4602, $800.00.

4702 Magazine Stand, 4 shelves, 26" x 13" x 31", EX, numbered, $1,000.00.

4703 Magazine Stand, 4 shelves, 26" x 13" x 40", VG, Paper label, $850.00.

4706 Magazine Stand, 4 shelves, 3 vertical spindles, 27" x 13" x 40", VG, Quaint metal tray, signed, $1,500.00.

4706 Magazine Stand, original finish, 39" x 26" x 12", EX, Quaint decal, $650.00.

4743 Magazine Stand, 5 shelves, 14" x 11" x 42", VG, $1,000.00.

4743 Magazine Stand, 5 open shelves, 5 graduated shelves, 14" x 13" x 42", VG, $750.00.

Magazine Stand, 5 shelves, cutouts to sides & back, 14" x 12" x 49", VG, $950.00.

Magazine Stand, spindled sides, 4 shelves, 39" x 26" x 12", G, $1,100.00.

Magazine Stand, mahogany, 43" x 19½" x 15", VG, Quaint tag, $1,265.00.

Magazine Stand, original finish, 46½" x 15½" x 12½", VG, Quaint tag, $1,380.00.

Magazine Stand, spindled sides, 4 shelves, 40" x 26" x 30", G, $1,100.00.

Stickley Brothers magazine stand, with slatted sides and back, gallery top, and four shelves. 40" x 26½" x 13". $850.00.

Not Shown

7308 Mirror, rectangular, 2 vertical slats, iron hooks, 38" x 21", VG, numbered, $850.00.

7507 Mirror (hall), rectangular, tenon construction at all sides, 39" x 27", EX, numbered, $700.00.

7577 Mirror (hall), tenon construction, iron hooks, 44" x 32", VG, Quaint metal tag, $1,100.00.

9032½ Mirror (shaving), 20" x 20" x 7", VG, $500.00.

Mirror (shaving), 20" x 19" x 7", AVG+, branded, decal, $300.00.

Mirror (hall), cut-out frame, 2 iron hooks, 3 copper hooks, 28¼" x 53", G, $550.00.

Mirror (hall), 2 large hooks on each side, 3 small hooks on bottom, 34" x 23", EX, Quaint metal tag, $550.00.

Mirror (hall), iron hooks & chain supports, 41" x 32", EX, $1,100.00.

Stickley Brothers wall mirror, with mortised construction and replaced beveled glass. Refinished, good condition, 21" x 24". $550.00.

Not Shown

631 Morris Rocker, flat arms, through-tenons, rope seat, 22" x 27" x 37", EX, Quaint tag, $1,200.00.

782½ Morris Rocker, adjustable back w/wooden pegs, 29" x 34" x 41", EX, $800.00.

Morris Chair, adjustable back w/wooden pegs, 29" x 33" x 43", VG, $700.00.

Morris Chair, horizontal seat rail, tenon construction, 31" x 38" x 36", VG, $1,800.00.

Morris Rocker, open arms, spring seat, 39" x 30" x 34½", EX, paper label, $1,600.00.

Parlor Sets

Not Shown

Parlor set (3 pieces, two armchairs and settee), vertical backseats to each, turned legs, loose cushions, chairs are 36½" x 26½" x 22½", settee is 36½" x 50¾" x 22¾", G, Quaint metal tag, $1,400.00 – 1,900.00.

Stickley Brothers 3-piece parlor set consisting of two armchairs and a settee, each with vertical backslats, turned legs, cotton-upholstered loose cushion, and original finish. Quaint metal tag, as-is condition, chairs are 36½" x 26½" x 22½", settee is 36½" x 50¾" x 22¾". Settee has one broken arm. $1,400.00 – 1,600.00.

Not Shown

131 Plant Stand, square top, cruciform leg base, 14" x 14" x 34", VG, $1,300.00.

131 Plant Stand, square top, cruciform leg base, 14" x 34", VG, $750.00.

133 Plant Stand, square top, footed base, 13" x 13" x 34", VG, Quaint Metal Tag, $700.00.

135 Plant Stand, overhanging top, cross-stretcher base, 14" x 34", VG, Quaint tag, numbered, $750.00.

183 Plant Stand, original finish, 34" x 13" x 13", VG, Quaint metal tag, $1,150.00.

Plant Stand, 15" x 18", VG, $500.00.

Plant Stand, pedestal, square top & base, pyramid feet, 34" x 13", EX, Quaint metal tag, stencil number, $1,700.00.

Stickley Brothers plant stand, with square overhanging top, apron, vertical side slats, stretchers mortised through the legs, very good original finish, and Quaint metal tag. Good conditon, 34½" x 17" x 17". $1,400.00.

Stickley Brothers ladder-back rocker, with open arms, seat cushion reupholstered in brown vinyl, original finish, and paper label. Very good condition, 33½" x 28½" x 31½". $900.00.

Stickley Brothers rocker, with four vertical backslats and open arms with long corbels. Good condition, 37¼" x 28" x 31½". $325.00 – 350.00.

Stickley Brothers spindled-back rocker, with flat paddle arms, slatted seat support, and original finish. Missing cushions, branded "568," good condition, 36" x 32" x 36½". $1,300.00.

Not Shown

298 Rocker, 4 vertical backslats, saddle seat, 39" w, G, $325.00.

379–415 Rocker, wing back, 37" x 30" x 30", VG, $800.00.

715 Rocker, drop arms, 5 slats to back, 29" x 30" x 32", VG, Quaint tag, $850.00.

728 Rocker, 6 vertical slats to back, 6 slats under each arm, 27" x 26" x 38", VG, numbered, signed, $850.00.

859½ Rocker and Armchair, original finish, rocker is 32" x 27" x 24", armchair is 35" x 27" x 24", VG, $1,100.00.

3819 Rocker, original finish, 35" x 29" x 26", VG, $800.00.

Rocker, bent arm, 2 horizontal slats to back, 27" x 22" x 39", VG, Quaint metal tag, $1,200.00.

Rocker, large, 5 slats under each arm, 29" x 34" x 30", VG, $2,100.00.

Rocker, 29" x 34" x 40".

Rocker, 2 wide vertical slats to back & arms, 32" x 36" x 33", VG, $2,000.00.

Rocker, inlaid, 35½" x 25½" x 20½", EX, $1,750.00.

Rocker, open arms, crestrail, 5 vertical backslats, 36" x 27" x 27", G, Quaint metal tag, branded mark, $475.00.

Rocker, tall back, 6 backslats, corbels, 37" x 27" x 28¼", G, $450.00.

Rocker, 6 vertical slats to back & sides, 37½" x 29" x 31¼", G, $450.00.

Rocker, refinished, 38" x 27½" x 28½", G, $1,035.00.

Rocker, concave crestrail, 42" x 27" x 29", G, $175.00.

Rocker, tall back, 43½" x 29½" x 25", VG, $1,265.00.

Rocker, open arms, crestrail, 5 vertical backslats, 36" x 32" x 36½", G, Quaint metal tag, branded mark, $475.00.

L. & J. G. Stickley
Furniture Company
(1902 – present)

The L. & J. G. Stickley Furniture Company was founded in 1902, by Gustav Stickley's two younger brothers Leopold and John George Stickley. These two brothers sold a wide variety of furniture, including bedroom and office furniture (which Gustav Stickley only produced on a limited basis). Among their customers was Harley Bradley of Kanakee, Illinois, whose house had been designed by the famous Frank Lloyd Wright. Although John Ayers made much of the furniture designed for Bradley's home, other pieces of furniture came from L. & J. G. Stickley and are still in the home today.

All furniture made by the company contained a decal and "Handcraft" or "Onondaga Shops" along with each brothers initials. From 1904 until 1906, the decal read, "The Onondage Shops/L. & J. G. Stickley/Fayetteville, New York." In latter years, the company adopted a new mark, which featured a woodworker's clamp that read, "L. & J. G. Stickley/Handcraft/Trade Mark" in the form of a red decal or a brand. It continued to be used until 1912. In that year, another mark was chosen — a red and yellow decal that sat within a rectangular reserve and read, "The work of/L. & J.G. Stickley." The last L. & J. G. Stickley Arts and Crafts furniture mark was introduced in 1918, following the termination of their brother Gustav Stickley's firm. It featured a conjoined woodworker's clamp and joiner's compass, and let the public know that the brothers now owned a controlling interest in Gustav Stickley's factory. The new red and yellow circular decal said, "Stickley/Handcraft Craftsmen/Syracuse & Fayetteville, N.Y."

The company first operated under the name of Onondaga Shops and was originally located in Fayetteville, New York, not far from brother Gustav's factory. The L. and J. G. Stickley Company is still in business today and is located in Manlius, New York, where much of its original in Colonial Williamsburg–style furniture is reproduced.

L & J. G. Stickley "Onondaga Shops" armchair, with five vertical slats, arched crestrail, recovered laced brown leather cushions, and original finish. Good condition, 39" x 27½" x 24". $5,500.00 – 7,500.00.

L. & J. G. Stickley armchair, with original tacked-on leather seat and back, and original dark finish. Good condition, 36" x 25" x 23". $3,000.00 – 4,000.00.

L. & J. G. Stickley drop armchair, with slats to the seat, corbels, and green leather drop-in spring seat and back cushion. Fine condition, waxed finish, "Handcraft" label, 41" x 32¼" x 33". $5,000.00.

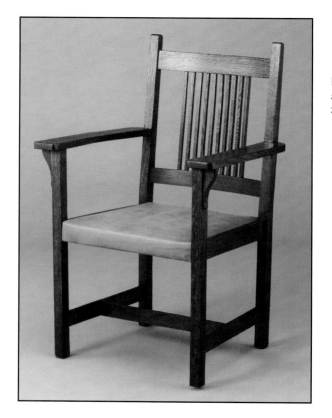

L & J. G. Stickley spindled-back armchair, with open arms, corbels, and seat recovered in leather. Refinished, very good condition, 38½" x 24½" x 21". $600.00.

Set of three L. & J. G. Stickley ladder-back armchairs, with flaring armrests, corseted leg rails, plank seats, and original finish (two chairs are overcoated). Some looseness, "the work of" decal, fair condition, 37¾" x 26½" x 19½". $800.00.

Set of four L & J. G. Stickley armchairs, with curved crestrails, five vertical backslats each, and tan leather drop-in seat cushions. Refinished, excellent condition, 34½" x 21" x 27". $2,700.00.

L & J. G. Stickley hall chair, with five vertical blackslats, open arms, long corbels, black leather-upholstered seat cushion, overcoated original finish, and minor looseness. "The work of" brand, very good condition, 47" x 28" x 23". $1,900.00.

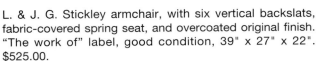

L. & J. G. Stickley armchair, with six vertical backslats, fabric-covered spring seat, and overcoated original finish. "The work of" label, good condition, 39" x 27" x 22". $525.00.

L & J. G. Stickley armchair and rocker set, with four vertical backslats each and drop-in seat cushions. New finish and upholstery, good condition, 39½" x 26" x 22". $1,200.00.

Not Shown

20 Armchair, 4 horizontal slats to back, 31" x 30" x 42", VG, "work of" decal, signed, $1,100.00.

388 Armchair, leather back & seat, 27" x 42" x 37", VG, "Handcraft decal", n/s, $4,250.00.

420 Armchair, 4 horizontal slats to back, arched seat rail, 31" x 30" x 42", VG, "work of decal", signed, $1,100.00.

422 Armchair, V-back over 6 vertical slats, 38" x 28" x 21", G, $400.00.

426 Armchair, 4 wide slats under each arm, 4 slats to back, 28" x 30" x 30", VG, $5,000.00.

450 Armchair, 6 vertical backslats, corbels, 29" x 25" x 40", VG, $650.00.

450 Armchair, 6 vertical backslats, corbels, 39½" x 28" x 22¾", G, $600.00 - 800.00.

750 Armchair, inverted V-back, center slat, 27" x 22" x 39", VG, $450.00.

802 Armchair, ladder-back, drop-in spring seat, 37" x 25½" x 20½", G, "work of" decal, signed, $600.00.

810 Armchair, 5 backslats, peaked rail, G, $400.00.

814 Armchair, 5 slats to back & under seat, drop-in cushion, 27" x 21" x 45", VG, $2,100.00.

816 Armchair, 6 vertical slats to back, 27" x 21" x 39", VG, "work of" decal, signed, $600.00.

816 Armchair, 6 vertical backslats, long corbels, refinished, 39" x 27" x 21", G, branded mark, signed, $350.00.

818 Armchair, ladder-back, open arms, long corbels, 39" x 28" x 23", FR, stenciled "818," $200.00 – 300.00.

850 Armchair, 6 slats to back, 6 slats under arm, 31" x 30" x 40", EX, "Onondaga Shops", $1,900.00.

Armchair, 8 spindles to back, 18" x 16" x 40", EX, "Handcraft" decal, $1,100.00.

Armchair, hard leather, 24" x 19" x 40", VG, $475.00.

Armchair, 6 vertical slats, drop-in seat, 27" x 22" x 13", EX, branded signature, $800.00.

Armchair, mahogany, deepseated, crestrail, 34¾" x 31½" x 29½", G, "Onondaga Shops", $950.00.

Armchair, ladder-back, 36¾" x 25½" x 20¼", as-is condition, conjoined symbols label, $350.00.

Armchair, refinished, replaced leather, 37" x 29" x 21", EX, "Onondaga Shops", $650.00 – 850.00.

Armchair, original finish, 40" x 28" x 23", F, $575.00

Armchair, drop arm, corbels, drop-in seat, 41" x 32¼" x 33", F, "Handcraft" label, $5,500.00.

Armchair, vertical slats, corbels, drop-in seat, 45" x 27" x 22", VG, "Handcraft" decal, $350.00 – 450.00.

Chairs (set of 7), 8 spindles to backs, 18" x 16" x 40", VG, "Handcraft" decal, $4,750.00.

L. & J. G. Stickley three-quarter size bed, with tall and tapering posts, vertical slats to headboard and footboard, slatted mattress supports, and good original finish. "The work of" decal, good condition, 50¾" x 80" x 46". $2,000.00.

L. & J. G. Stickley full-size bed, with raised posts, 12 vertical slats each to headboard and footboard, side rails, and original finish to part of the bed. Repegged, conjoined symbols label, good condition, headboard 50" x 57". $2,600.00.

Not Shown

83 Bed (¾ size), arched apron, double panel construction, 46" x 51", EX, $2,000.00.

92 Bed (single), wide slat at center of each end, 2 smaller slats on each side, 44" x 46", EX, "work of" decal, signed, $2,600.00.

92 Bed, tall tapered posts, 7 slats, wide center slat, 58" x 44", EX, signed, $10,000.00.

92 Bed (single), wide slat at center of each end, 80" x 50", EX, "work of" decal, signed, $325.00.

Bed (¾ size), tall tapering posts, vertical slat, 50¾" x 80" x 46", G, "work of" decal, signed, $2,000.00.

Bed (full), raised posts, and 12 vertical slats, 50" x 57", G, conjoined symbols label, $2,600.00.

292 Daybed, 4 vertical slats between angled posts, 80" x 30" x 28", VG, "Handcraft" decal, $2,800.00.

295 Daybed, angled form, 5 slats to head & foot, 72" x 28" x 22", VG, $950.00.

922 Daybed, vertical headrest, 3 wide slats, 72" x 27" x 28", VG, "Onondaga Shops," $2,500.00.

Daybed, slanted headrest, 5 vertical slats, 76" x 30" x 26", VG, "Handcraft" decal, $900.00.

L. & J. G. Stickley double-door bookcase, with gallery top, 12 panes to each door, keyed through-tenon sides, hammered-copper pulls, excellent original finish, fine quartersawn wood throughout, and good patina on hardware. "The work of" brand, excellent condition, 55" x 49" x 12". $9,000.00.

L. & J. G. Stickley single-door bookcase, with gallery top, 16 panes, and keyed through-tenons. Refinished, "Handcraft" mark, excellent condition, 55¼" x 29¾" x 12". $9,000.00.

L. & J. G. Stickley double-door bookcase, with gallery top, 12 panes per door, three shelves, keyed through-tenons on the sides, and excellent original medium finish. "The work of" decal, excellent condition, 54½" x 49" x 12". $5,500.00.

L. & J. G. Stickley double-door bookcase, with gallery top, eight panes per door, through-tenons, copper pulls, and very good cleaned original finish. "The work of" decal, very good condition, 56" x 39½" x 12¾". $5,000.00.

L. & J. G. Stickley single-door bookcase (model 327), with gallery top, 16-pane door, hammered-copper V-pull, keyed through-tenons, and excellent refinish. Excellent condition, 57" x 36" x 12". $6,000.00 – 7,000.00.

L. & J .G. Stickley bookcase, with gallery top, 16 glass panes, and keyed through-tenons. Refinished, very good condition, 56½" x 39½" x 12". $4,500.00.

L. & J. G. Stickley double-door bookcase, with gallery top, 12 panes to each door, hammered-copper pulls, top and base mortised through sides, good original finish, and "Handcraft" decal. Good condition, 55" x 52" x 12". $6,000.00.

L. & J. G. Stickley double-door bookcase, with gallery top, 12 panes to each door, hammered-copper pulls, top and base mortised through sides, and "the work of" decal. Very good condition, 55" x 52" x 12". $6,500.00. This is the same style of bookcase as in the above photo. The only difference is that this bookcase has a "work of" decal, and the one in the above photo has a "Handcraft" decal.

L. & J. G. Stickley "Onondaga Shops" chestnut open bookcase, with gallery top, chamfered back and sides, and three shelves. Good condition, 50" x 36" x 12". $2,200.00 – 2,500.00.

L. & J. G. Stickley double-door bookcase, with gallery top and original finish with old overcoat. Signed, "work of" decal, very good condition, 55" x 50" x 11½". $4,600.00. *Photo courtesy of Craftsman Auctions.*

L. & J. G. Stickley "Onondaga Shops" single-door bookcase (model 327). Excellent condition, refinished, 57" x 36" x 12". $6,000.00 – 7,000.00.

Not Shown

328½ Bookcase, 2 doors, original finish, 57" x 49" x 19", AVG, $7,000 – 9,000.00.

331 Bookcase, 3 doors, 12 panes per door, copper hardware, 74" x 12" x 57", VG, "Onondaga Shops," numbered, $20,000.00.

638 Bookcase, 2 doors, arched base, 48" x 14" x 48", EX, conjoined symbols label, $3,750.00.

641 Bookcase, original finish, 34" x 12" x 57", EX, "Handcraft" decal, signed, $5,500.00.

641 Bookcase, single door, 8 panes, board back, 40" x 12" x 55", EX, "Handcraft" decal, signed, $6,500.00.

641 Bookcase, single door, 16 panels of glass, 40" x 12" x 58", EX, "Handcraft" decal, signed, $6,500.00.

642 Bookcase, through-tenon top & bottom, 30" x 12" x 55", VG, "Handcraft" decal, $1,200.00.

643 Bookcase, 2 doors, 8 panes per door, 40" x 12" x 55", VG, "work of" decal, signed, $4,500.00.

643 Bookcase, 2 doors, copper hardware, 55" x 39", VG, $6,000.00.

645 Bookcase, 2 doors, 12 panes per door, original finish, 48" x 12" x 56", VG, $6,500.00.

645 Bookcase, 2 doors, 12 panes per door, 52" x 12" x 55", VG, $6,500.00.

646 Bookcase, open, chamfered back, 49" x 12" x 55", VG, $2,200.00.

647 Bookcase, 3 doors, 12 panes per door, 9 shelves, 55" x 72", EX, signed, $16,000.00.

647 Bookcase, 3 doors, 12 panes per door, 73" x 12" x 58", EX, $10,000.00.

652 Bookcase, single door, peaked gallery, 22" x 11" x 51", EX, $3,500.00.

Bookcase, single door, 16 panes, copper hardware, 39" x 12" x 55", EX, "Handcraft" decal, $5,000.00.

Bookcase, 2 doors, 12 panes per door, copper hardware, 55" x 53" x 12", EX, $7,000.00.

Bookcase, 2 doors, 12 panes per door, 56" x 49" x 11½", G, "Onondaga Shops," $1,200.00.

L.& J. G. Stickley chest (model 99), with four drawers, arched backsplash and apron, paneled sides, round wooden pulls, original finish, and "Handcraft" decal. Very good condition, 37" x 48" x 22". $3,500.00.

L & J. G. Stickley chest of drawers, with overcoated finish. Excellent condition, 40" x 38" x 18½". $1,840.00. *Photo courtesy of Craftsman Auctions.*

L. & J. G. Stickley chest of drawers, with mirror. Refinished, excellent condition, signed, "work of" decal, 69" x 38" x 18". $2,300.00. *Photo courtesy of Craftsman Auctions.*

Not Shown

90 Chest of Drawers, 2 half drawers over 4 full, 34" x 20" x 53", VG, "Handcraft" decal, $1,500.00.

94 Chest of Drawers, 9 drawers, wooden knobs, 32" x 19" x 53", VG, "Handcraft" decal, $3,750.00.

94 Chest of Drawers, 9 drawers, wooden knobs, paneled sides, 39" x 19" x 53", VG, "Handcraft" decal, signed, $5,500.00.

China Cabinets

L. & J. G. Stickley china cabinet (model 746), with overhanging top, glass panel doors with mullioned tops, hammered-copper hardware, arched toeboards, and "Handcraft" label. Average condition, 62" x 44" x 16". $6,000.00.

L. & J. G. Stickley double-door china cabinet, with gallery top, six panes per door, hammered-copper pulls, arched apron, excellent original finish, and conjoined symbols mark. Very good condition, 55" x 47½" x 15". $3,500.00.

L. & J. G. Stickley double-door china cabinet, with back-splash, eight panes to each door, hammered-copper pulls, and good original finish. Legs removed, "the work of" brand, fair condition, 50" x 36" x 14". $2,600.00.

L. & J. G. Stickley double-door china cabinet, with arched gallery top, six glass panes per door, copper hardware, arched toeboard, three interior shelves, original finish, and branded mark inside door. Excellent condition, 55" x 47¾" x 15". $3,500.00.

L. & J. G. Stickley double-door china cabinet, with overhanging top, six small glass panes over large panes on doors and sides, three adjustable shelves, hammered-copper pulls, and new finish. Very good condition, 62" x 44" x 16". $4,750.00.

L. & J. G. Stickley double-door china cabinet, with gallery top, six panes per door, hammered-copper pulls, arched apron, excellent original finish, new metal slide doorstop, and conjoined symbols mark. Very good condition, 55" x 47½" x 15". $3,500.00.

L. & J. G. Stickley double-door china cabinet, with overhanging rectangular top, leaded glass panes over single panes on doors and sides, three interior shelves, good original finish, and "Handcraft" decal. Good condition, 66" x 44" x 16". $8,000.00.

L. & J. G. Stickley double-door china cabinet, with paneled back, six glass panes to each door and three to each side, arched toeboard, and excellent original finish. Numbered 285/728, in black. Excellent condition, 54" x 47½" x 15". $6,000.00.

L. & J. G. Stickley single-door china cabinet, with paneled back, nine glass panes to door and three to each side, arched toeboards, two interior shelves, excellent original finish, and "the work of" decal. Excellent condition, 55" x 34" x 15". $4,750.00.

L. & J. G. Stickley double-door china cabinet, with overhanging top, mullioned panes over long glass panels on doors and sides, one fixed interior plate shelf, and two adjustable shelves. Refinished, very good condition, 62" x 46" x 16". $4,750.00.

L. & J. G. Stickley china cabinet (model 746). Average condition, refinished, signed, "Handcraft" label, 62" x 44" x 16". $6,000.00.

Photo courtesy of Craftsman Auctions.

Not Shown

727 China Cabinet, single door, 9 panes, 34" x 15" x 55", M, paper label, signed, $4,500.00.

728 China Cabinet, 2 doors, 9 panes per door, stationary shelves, 48" x 15" x 55", EX, $3,750.00.

729 China Cabinet, 2 doors, 12 panes per door, 50" x 17" x 70", EX, "Handcraft" decal, signed, $45,000.00.

746 China Cabinet, 2 doors, glass sides, 6 panes per door, 40" x 15" x 62", EX, "work of" decal, signed, $6,500.00.

746 China Cabinet, 2 doors, 12 panes per door, copper pulls, 44" x 16" x 62", EX, "work of" decal, signed, $6,500.00.

746 China Cabinet, 2 doors, glass sides, 12 panes per door, adjustable shelves, 44" x 16" x 69", EX, "Handcraft" decal, $6,000.00.

761 China cabinet, single door, 3 shelves, copper hardware, 36" x 16" x 60", EX, "Handcraft" decal, $5,500.00.

China Cabinet, single drawer over 2 doors, 32" x 22" x 38", VG, "work of" decal, signed, $2,500.00.

89 Costumer, single tapered post on base, 25" x 72", EX, "work of" decal, signed, $1,400.00.

Costumer, wide double pole, 6 brass hooks, 32" x 72", VG, "work of" decal, signed, $1,900.00.

L. & J. G. Stickley coat rack, with divided top compartment, trestle base with shoe feet, original finish, and "the work of" decal. Excellent condition, 72" x 102" x 22". $3,500.00.

L. & J. G. Stickley costumer, four corbeled shoe feet and original brass hooks, excellent original finish, and "the work of" label. Excellent condition, 73" x 24" x 24". $1,200.00.

L. & J. G. Stickley rare and tall case clock, with beveled overhanging top, large acid-etched copper face, glass panel door with copper hardware; brass works, weights, and pendulum; and excellent original finish, color condition, and wood choice. Marked on face of clock, "L. & J.G. Stickley, Fayetteville, New York." "Handcraft" decal, excellent condition, 80½" x 21½" x 13". $28,000.00.

L. & J. G. Stickley hall bench, with hinged seat compartment, columnar vertical slats to back and arms, long corbels under the apron, original finish, minor edge wear, and "Handcraft" decal. Excellent condition, 37" x 42" x 18". $6,000.00.

L. & J. G. Stickley tall clock, model 91, signed inside lower cabinet, excellent condition, original finish, original patina on hardware and clock face, 78" x 19½" x 12". $15,000.00 – 25,000.00. *Photo courtesy of Craftsman Auctions.*

L. & J. G. Stickley trapezoidal shelf clock (model 85), original finish. Signed, "Handcraft" label, mint condition, 22" x 16" x 8". $10,000.00. *Photo courtesy of Craftsman Auctions.*

Not Shown

Mantle Clock, retangular case, copper face, 16" x 8" x 22", EX, "work of" decal, signed, $8,500.00.

L. & J. G. Stickley desk, with single blind drawer, slatted bookshelves to each side, and branded mark. Good condition, 39" x 42" x 28". $500.00 – 700.00.

L. & J. G. Stickley desk, with single blind drawer, two bookshelves (one on either side), and single slats to front and back. Refinished, "the work of" brand. Good condition, 30" x 42" x 27½". $800.00 – 1,200.00.

Not Shown

395 Desk, ash, slant front, drop front, splayed legs, 33" x 15" x 48", VG, "Onondaga Shops," $1,700.00.

395 Desk, ash, slant front, brass escutcheon, drop front, 36" x 15" x 48", VG, $850.00.

400 Desk, single drawer over kneehole opening, 2 drawers w/copper pulls, 42" x 60" x 30", VG, "work of" decal, signed, $1,000.00.

500 Desk, single drawer over kneehole, 2 drawers on each side, copper hardware, 42" x 26" x 29", VG, "work of" decal, signed, $650.00.

501 Desk, 2 drawers on each side, through-tenon construction, copper hardware, 42" x 26" x 29", VG, "work of" decal, signed, $950.00.

503 Desk, single drawer flanked by bookshelves on sides, 44" x 38" x 29", VG, "work of" decal, signed, $550.00.

512 Deck, rectangular top, single drawer, 2 shelves on each side, 40" x 26" x 30", VG, "work of" decal, signed, $1,000.00.

565 Desk (table), single drawer, copper hardware, 42" x 28" x 29", VG, "Handcraft" decal, $2,000.00.

601 Desk (writing), original finish, 35" x 34" x 20", VG, $920.00.

609 Desk, two drawers, arched gallery, letter holders at side, 44" x 22" x 37", VG, "work of" decal, signed, $1,300.00.

660 Desk, fall front, 2 drawers over 1, 29" x 17" x 40", VG, "work of" decal, signed, $1,000.00.

661 Desk, drop front, 44½" x 42" x 20", $1,667.00.

662 Desk, double-door cabinet top w/12 panes, copper hardware, 42" x 31" x 72", EX, "work of" decal, signed, $4,500.00.

Desk (writing), refinished, 30" x 45½" x 29½", VG, "guaranteed furn" label, $1,150.00.

Desk, 10 spindles to each side, 2 drawers, refinished, 36" x 20" x 29", VG, $2,600.00.

Desk (partners'), leather top, single drawer, 2 shelves on each side, 48" x 30" 30", VG, $2,200.00.

Chair, mahongany, 37" x 16" x 45", AVG, branded signature, $325.00.

L. & J. G. Stickley extenision dining table, with circular top, five posts to pedestal base, and shoe feet. Price includes four 12" leaves in storage rack. Good original finish, normal wear to top, "the work of" decal, very good condition, 29" x 48". $3,000.00.

L. & J. G. Stickley hexagonal dining table with arched apron and cross-stretchers with faceted center finial and keyed through the legs. Refinished, "Handcraft" label, very good condition, 29¼" x 55" x 48". $2,200.00.

L. & J. G. Stickley lunch table (model 539), 1910 era, with overhanging circular top and arched stretchers with through-tenons. This table originally came from the Asbury Park Elks Club in New Jersey. Worn original finish to base, new finish to top, branded, "the work of" decal. Very good condition, 29" x 42". $1,200.00 – 1,600.00.

L. & J. G. Stickley extension dining table, with circular top and cross-stretchers mortised through the legs. Worn original finish, without leaves, metal tag, fair condition, 29½" x 48½". $1,700.00.

L. & J. G. Stickley luncheon table, with rectangular top and apron, original finish to base, and top that has been refinished and cut down. "Handcraft" label, good condition, 30" x 48" x 35". $1,250.00 – 1,750.00.

L. & J. G. Stickley dining side chairs, with arched vertical backslats, drop-in spring seats covered in new green leather, good new finish, and "Handcraft" label. Very good condition, 37½" x 17" x 17½". $2,900.00.

L. & J. G. Stickley drop-leaf occasional table, with circular top, footed base, and replaced stretchers. Refinished, good condition, 30" x 28". $700.00 – 800.00.

L. & J. G. Stickley round oak dining table (model 713), with four leaves and restored finish. Excellent condition, 30" x 48". $2,350.00.

L & J. G. Stickley drop-leaf gate-leg table, with shoe feet. Refinished, "the work of" brand, very good condition, 30" x 41½". $3,750.00.

L. & J. G. Stickley extension dining table, with circular top, pedestal base, shoe feet, four leaves, and original finish. Good condition, 30" x 48". $3,750.00.

L. & J. G. Stickley round oak dining table, with two leaves, base in original finish with overcoat, and refinished top. Good condition, 29" x 48". $1,495.00. *Photo courtesy of Craftsman Auctions.*

L. & J. G. Stickley dining table, with circular top and apron, arched cross-stretchers with through-tenons, and "Handcraft" decal. Refinished, fair condition, 29" x 48". $950.00.

L. & J. G. Stickley dining table, with circular top, serpentine apron, cross-stretchers keyed through shaped plank legs and topped by a wooden finial, original finish to base, and refinished top. Excellent condition, "the work of" tag, 30" x 72". $11,000.00.

Not Shown

800 Dining Chairs (5 #800, 1 #802 armchair), 18" x 17" x 37", VG, $2,500.00.

800 Dining Chairs (set of 6), 36" x 18" x 17", EX, branded signature, $4,325.00.

802 Dining Chairs (set of 5), drop-in cushions, 26" x 20" x 37", VG, $2,500.00.

804 Dining Chairs (set of 6, 5 sides and 1 arm), side chairs are 19" x 18" x 37", armchair is 26" x 21" x 37", VG, "Handcraft" decal, $1,600.00.

820 Dining Chairs (pair), 36" x 19½" x 17", G, "Handcraft" decal, $400.00.

940 Dining Chair, (set of 6), 3 vertical slats to back, 18" x 16" x 36", VG, "work of" decal, signed, $2,200.00.

Dining chairs (set of 6), 3 slats to back, plank seats, 17" x 16" x 34", VG, "Handcraft" decal, $700.00.

Dining chairs (set of 6, 5 sides and 1 arm), 3 horizontal slats to back, 18" x 17" x 37", EX, "work of" decal, signed, $3,500.00.

709 & 718 Dining Room Set (#709 sideboard, #718 table, chairs), EX, "work of" decal, signed, $8,050.00.

716 Dining Table (prairie design), circular top, 42" x 30", VG, "work of" decal, signed, $2,100.00.

717 Dining Table, large round top, center pedestal, 3 leaves, 60" x 30", EX, "work of" decal, signed, $6,000.00.

720 Dining Table, round top, 5 tapered legs, 48" x 30", EX, branded signature, $3,500.00.

722 Dining Table, round top, 4 leaves, legs drop down for expansion, 48" x 29", EX, "Handcraft" decal, $750.00.

Dining table, round oak, 2 leaves, refinished, 29" x 48", G, $1,495.00.

Dining Table, circular top, 30" x 72", EX, "work of" decal, signed, $11,000.00.

Dining Table, drop leaf, oval top, 64" x 45" x 30", VG, "Handcraft" decal, $1,400.00.

Dressers

L. & J. G. Stickley hat box dresser, with backsplash, two cabinet doors over two small drawers, three large drawers, and wooden pulls. Refinished, "the work of" decal, very good condition, 49¾" x 36" x 28". $3,500.00.

L. & J. G. Stickley dresser, with arched backsplash and toeboards, paneled sides, two-over-three-drawer configuration, circular wooden pulls, original finish, and "Handcraft" decal. Good condition, 43¾" x 34" x 20¼". $2,100.00.

L. & J. G. Stickley dresser, with pivoting mirror, two small drawers over three large ones, circular wooden pulls, arched toeboard. Refinished, "the work of" decal, branded numbers, good condition, 69½" x 38" x 19". $2,400.00.

Not Shown

90 Chiffonier, 2 small drawers over 4 large, 49¾" x 42" x 18¼", EX, $4,000.00.

102 Chiffonier, 2 cabinet doors over 4 drawers, wooden knobs, 36" x 18" x 50", EX, $2,700.00.

111 Chiffonier, chest w/2 paneled doors, 48" x 40" x 19", VG, $2,900.00.

81 Dresser, 3 drawers over 2, wooden knobs, mirror, 44" x 21" x 67", VG, $1,600.00.

101 Dresser, 3 small drawers over 2 large, mirror, 45" x 21" x 67", EX, "work of" decal, signed, $1,900.00.

Dresser, two small drawers over two large, paneled sides, mirror, wooden knobs, 42" x 24" x 67", EX, $1,200.00.

87 Dressing Table, 2 drawers, wooden knobs, lower shelf, paneled sides, 44" x 22" x 55", VG, "Handcraft," $1,700.00.

Night Stand, 2 drawers, wooden knobs, 20" x 14" x 30", EX, $1,000.00.

Wardrobe, paneled cabinet, single door, hanging rod, 26" x 21" x 74", VG, "work of" decal, signed, $2,200.00.

L. & J. G. Stickley drink stand, with circular top, circular lower shelf over cross-stretchers, refinished top, and excellent original finish to base. Excellent condition, 29¾" x 18". $1,000.00.

L. & J. G. Stickley drink stand, with circular copper-covered overhanging top, circular apron, cross-stretchers, and original finish. This drink stand originally came from the Asbury Park Elks Club in New Jersey. Conjoined label, excellent condition, 28" x 18". $2,400.00.

L. & J. G. Stickley drink stand, with circular copper-covered overhanging top and circular apron. One cross-stretcher is missing. This stand came from the Asbury Park Elks Club New Jersey. As-is condition, conjoined symbols label, 28¾" x 18". $500.00.

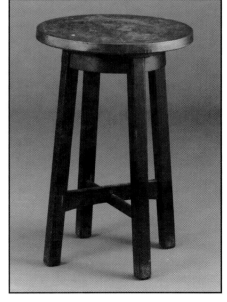

L. & J. G. Stickley drink stand, with circular copper-covered overhanging top, circular apron, and cross-stretchers. This stand came from the Asbury Park Elks Club in New Jersey. Overcoated finish, as-is condition, one stretcher has been replaced, 28¾" x 18". $500.00. This model is identical to the one in the photo on the left.

Not Shown

22 Drink Stand, copper top, 18" x 28", AVG, branded signature, $1,250.00.

22 Drink Stand, round leather top, arched cross-stretchers, 18" x 29", EX, $3,250.00.

587 Drink Stand, refinished base, 15" x 28", VG, "Onondaga Shops," $850.00.

587 Drink Stand, refinished top, original finish to base, 16" x 27", VG, "work of" decal, signed, $700.00.

587 Drink Stand, 28", VG, "Onondaga Shops", $800.00.

   Drink Stand, circular copper top, flared legs, 28¼" x 18", EX, "Handcraft," $6,500.00.

L. & J. G. Stickley rectangular footstool, with arched sides, through-tenons, and replaced brown leather seat. Refinished, good condition, 15¾" x 20" x 13½". $950.00.

L. & J. G. Stickley footstool, with arched aprons. It is missing the original tacked-on leather seat, but the canvas support is still intact. "The work of" label, fair condition, 16" x 19" x 15". $500.00 – 600.00.

L. & J. G. Stickley footstool, with tacked-on brown leather top, arched sides, original finish, and new leather and tacks. "The work of" decal, good condition, 16" x 19¼" x 15¼". $750.00.

Not Shown

292 Footstool, 7 spindles at each side, 18" x 13" x 17", VG, $1,300.00.

391 Footstool, original hard leather & finish, 19" x 14" x 18", EX, "work of" decal, signed, $500.00.

394 Footstool, refinished, new leather, 19" x 15" x 16", G, $500.00.

397 Footstool, drop-in spring cushion, 20" x 14" x 16", EX, "work of" decal, signed, $400.00.

399 Footstool, collapsible stool, S-shaped slats, 16" x 16" x 17", VG, $1,200.00.

729 Footstool, leather seat, arched rail, 20" x 16" x 16", VG, $900.00.

1306 Footstool, refinished, 16" x 20" x 13½", AVG, conjoined symbols label, $250.00.

Footstool, original black leather finish, 9½" x 18" x 13", $300.00.

Footstool, straight rails, brown leather cushion, 38¼" x 17" x 17", G, $450.00.

Footstool, arched apron, 16" x 19" x 15", G, "work of" decal, signed, $500.00.

L. & J. G. Stickley double-drawer library table, with overhanging top, broad lower shelf mortised through the legs, hammered-copper pulls, good original finish to base, and "the work of" label. Good condition, 29½" x 48" x 30". $1,600.00.

L. & J. G. Stickley trestle library table, with rectangular top and lower shelf doubled-keyed through the legs. Refinished, excellent condition, 29" x 48" x 30". $2,200.00.

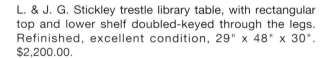

L. & J. G. Stickley double-drawer library table, with corbels, flat medial stretcher, wrought copper pulls, old refinish to top, base with excellent original finish, and "work of" decal. Excellent condition, 29" x 48" x 30". $2,200.00.

L. & J. G. Stickley trestle library table, with rectangular top, harp-shaped legs, and lower shelf. Good condition, 29" x 40" x 24¼". $1,700.00 - 2,000.00.

L. & J. G. Stickley double-drawer library table, with overhanging top, long corbels, copper pulls, mortised lower shelf and stretchers, refinished top, base overcoat, and "the work of" decal. Very good condition, 29" x 48" x 29½". $1,500.00.

L. & J. G. Stickley trestle library table, with rectangular top, lower shelf keyed through the sides, original finish, and "Handcraft" label. Excellent condition, 29¼" x 72" x 45¼". $3,750.00.

Not Shown

377 Library Table, single drawer, brass hardware, 48" x 30" x 30", VG, "Onondaga Shops," signed, $1,600.00.

511 Library Table, overhanging top, single drawer, lower shelf, 72" x 36" x 30", VG, conjoined symbols label, $3,750.00.

521 Library Table, single drawer, copper hardware, 42" x 28" x 29", EX, "Handcraft" decal, $1,700.00.

522 Library Table, single drawer, copper pulls, 42" x 28" x 29", EX, "Handcraft" decal, $1,200.00.

529 Library Table, single drawer, copper pulls, 42" x 28" x 29", EX, "work of" decal, signed, $1,300.00.

529 Library Table, rectangular top, single drawer, 48" x 28" x 29", VG, $700.00.

530 Library Table, single drawer, copper pulls, 36" x 24" x 29", VG, "work of" decal, signed, $900.00.

531 Library Table, refinished, 48" x 30" x 29", VG, conjoined symbols label, $1,200.00.

532 Library Table, original finish to base, 54" x 32" x 29", VG, "work of" decal, signed, $2,100.00.

597 Library Table, hidden drawer, original finish, 29" x 28½" x 40", EX, $1,050.00.

1152 Library Table, mahogany, 2 drawers, brass pulls, 48" x 30" x 29", VG, "Onondaga Shops," $1,900.00.

1282 Library Table, 2 drawers, 13 spindles to each side, 42" x 37" x 29", EX, "Onondaga Shops," $3,750.00.

Library Table, refinished, 29½" x 54" x 32", EX, $1,955.00.

L. & J. G. Stickley magazine stand, with overhanging top, broad side slats, arched stretchers, three shelves, and good original finish. Good condition, 44½" x 23¼" x 13". $1,700.00.

L. & J. G. Stickley "Onondaga Shops" magazine stand (model 346), with slatted sides, four shelves, and original finish. Very good condition, 42" x 21" x 12". $1,400.00.

L. & J. G. Stickley magazine stand, with four shelves and tapered sides. Refinished, good condition, 42" x 18" x 14½". $1,300.00.

L. & J. G. Stickley magazine stand, with slatted sides, arched apron, four shelves, original dark finish with over-coat, and "the work of" decal. Very good condition, 42" x 21" x12". $1,400.00.

Not Shown

41 Magazine Stand, rectangular top, 2 lower shelves, 36" x 12" x 30", VG, "work of" decal, signed, $1,600.00.

45 Magazine Stand, 4 shelves, arched support, 21" x 12" x 45", VG, "work of" decal, signed, $1,800.00.

45 Magazine Stand, 4 shelves, original finish, 19" x 12" x 46", VG, $1,800.00.

46 Magazine Stand, 4 shelves, 21" x 12" x 42", EX, $2,600.00.

47 Magazine Stand, tapered sides, tenon construction, 19" x 16" x 42", G, $750.00.

47 Magazine Stand, 4 shelves, arched toeboard, 20" x 14" x 42", VG, $850.00.

47 Magazine Stand, 4 shelves, slab sides, 18" x 15" x 42", G, $750.00.

Magazine Stand, 3 shelves, with single slats to each side, 24" x 13" x 44", EX, "work of" decal, signed, $2,600.00.

Magazine Stand, single board, each side, 30" x 36" x 12", G, "work of" decal, signed, $2,600.00.

Magazine Stand, with slatted sides, 4 shelves, 42" x 21" x 12", G, "work of" decal, signed, $1,100.00.

Magazine Rack, with gallery top, 4 shelves, 44¾" x 21" x 12", G, "work of" decal, signed, $2,100.00.

Magazine Stand, 4 shelves, paneled back, gallery top, 45" x 19" x 12", VG, "Handcraft" decal, $2,500.00.

Mirrors

Not Shown

65 Mirror (hall), curved top, 4 iron hooks, 40" x 27", VG, "work of" decal, signed, $2,500.00.

100 Mirror, arched top & bottom, original finish, 45" x 26", EX, $2,000.00.

Mirror (wall), 24½" x 55½", EX, "work of" decal, signed, $1,725.00.

Mirror (hall), peaked top & corbeled, 4 hooks, 40" x 24", EX, "work of" decal, signed, $2,300.00.

Miscellaneous

L. & J. G. Stickley log holder, with slatted sides and foundation, cut-out handles, tapered posts, arched toeboards, and original finish. Very good condition, 20" x 19¾" x 18¾". This log holder came from Leopold Stickley's estate sale, held in May 1982 in Syracuse, New York. It was estimated to bring between $2,500.00 and $3,500.00 at a May 1999 auction, and ended up selling for $2,900.00.

L. & J. G. Stickley cellarette, with single drawer, pull-out copper-lined shelf, lower cabinet with interior fittings, and "Handcraft" decal. Very good condition, 40" x 22" x 16". $3,000.00 – 4,000.00.

L. & J. G. Stickley rare Morris chair, with vertical slats, side panels carved with tabacco leaf motif, good original finish, and replaced seat foundation and cushions. Very good condition, 40" x 29¾". $3,000.00 – 4,000.00.

L. & J. G. Stickley Morris rocker, with vertical slats under flat arms, beveled rail upholstered in reproduction William Morris fabric, and a back cushion not shown in photo. Refinished, very good condition, 32" x 32" x 35". $3,250.00.

L. & J. G. Stickley flat Morris chair, with good original finish to base and tops of arms. Refinished, "Handcraft" label, very good condition, 41" x 35¼" x 31½". $2,000.00.

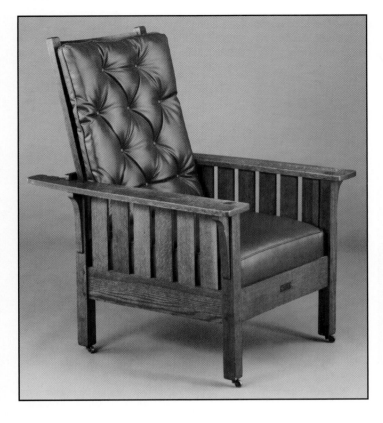

L. & J. G. Stickley Morris chair, with vertical slats under flat arms, corbels, new brown leather tufted cushions, and very good original finish. Very good condition, 43" x 32" x 35". $2,100.00.

L.& J. G. Stickley flat-arm Morris chair, with six vertical slats to sides, corbels, and drop-in spring seat recovered in brown vinyl. "The work of" decal, excellent condition, 40" x 32" x 35". $3,250.00.

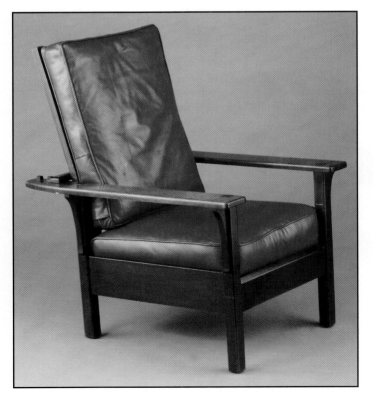

L & J. G. Stickley mahogany open-arm Morris chair, with long corbels and burgundy leather cushions. Good condition, 36" x 29½" x 35". $1,400.00.

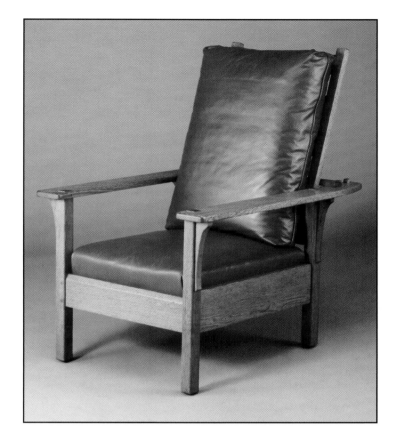

L. & J. G. Stickley open-arm Morris chair, with long corbels, new brown leather cushions, and "the work of" label. Good condition, 40" x 29¼" x 34¾". $1,700.00.

L. & J. G. Stickley open-arm Morris rocker, with long corbels, flat arms, four slats, drop-in spring seat and (not shown) back cushion recovered in blue fabric, worn original finish, "Handcraft" label, and "work of" decal. Fair condition, 39½" x 29½" x 34¾". $1,200.00.

L. & J. G. Stickley bow-arm Morris chair, with vertical slats under the arm, replaced upholsterery of green vinyl, and good original finish. "The work of" label, excellent condition, 38" x 34" x 41¾". $9,000.00.

L. & J. G. Stickley bow-arm Morris chair (model 416), with four short vertical slats to each side, long corbels, drop-in spring seat, replaced pivot pegs, new leather, and conjoined symbols label. Refinished, very good condition, 46" x 41" x 34". $8,000.00.

L. & J. G. Stickley bow-arm Morris chair (model 406), with original finish. Excellent condition, signed "Handcraft," 39" x 33½" x 40½". $23,000.00. *Photo courtesy of Craftsman Auctions.*

L. & J. G. Stickley Morris chair, with slats to floor, long corbels under the arms, original spring seat cushion reupholstered in ivory linen, and original finish. Very good condition, 38" x 34" x 37". $4,500.00.

L. & J. G. Stickley Morris chair (model 497), with original finish and leather. Excellent condition, signed "Handcraft," 41" x 32" x 36". $5,750.00. *Photo courtesy of Craftsman Auctions.*

L. & J. G. Stickley bow-arm Morris chair (model 406), with original finish. Signed "work of L. & J. G. Stickley," excellent condition, 41" x 34" x 41". $15,000.00 – 16,000.00. *Photo courtesy of Craftsman Auctions.*

Not Shown

108½ Morris Chair, early original finish, 40" x 32" x 36½", VG, "Onondaga Shops," $1,150.00.

410 Morris Chair, bent arms, 7 slats under each arm, 33" x 38" x 39", VG, $6,000.00.

410 Morris Chair, 7 wide slats under bent arms, 32" x 38" x 38", VG, "Handcraft" decal, signed, $6,000.00.

411 Morris chair, open arms, cushions, 32" x 36" x 42", EX, handcraft decal, signed, $3,750.00.

412 Morris Chair, paddle arms, long corbels, 35" x 39" x 39", EX, "Handcraft" decal, $7,000.00.

470 Morris chair, wide arms, 34" x 37" x 38", VG, "work of" decal, signed, $2,200.00.

470 Morris chair, corbels to legs, 34" x 37" x 40", EX, $2,600.00.

470 Morris Chair, 41" x 32" x 35½", AVG+, "Handcraft," signed, $2,500.00 – 3,500.00.

471 Morris Chair, 40" x 32" x 35", EX, "work of" decal, signed, $3,737.00.

471 Morris Chair, 4 horizontal slats to back, 32" x 36" x 41", VG, "Handcraft," $2,600.00.

497 Morris Chair, 5 slats under arm, leather cushions, 32" x 36" x 41", EX, "work of" decal, signed, $4,000.00.

498 Morris Chair, original finish, 34" x 38" x 40", VG, "Handcraft" decal, $2,800.00.

709 Morris Chair, paddle arms, 39" x 37" x 30", VG, $2,500.00 – 3,500.00.

762 Morris Chair, arched sides, rope seat, 42" x 43" x 33½", VG, $3,600.00.

798 Morris Chair, 5 slats under arms, 32" x 36" x 39", EX, $7,500.00.

830 Morris Chair, 29" x 35" x 41", VG, "work of" decal, signed, $950.00.

830 Morris Chair, original finish, VG, conjoined symbols label, $1,100.00 – 1,500.00.

831 Morris Rocker, long corbels under arms, G, "Handcraft" decal, $1,500.00.

Morris Chair, open arms, long corbels, 39½" x 29½" x 27", G, "work of" decal, signed, $1,500.00.

Morris Chair, 40" x 32" x 36", AVG, $2,450.00.

Morris Chair, open arms, 41" x 29½" x 35", FR, $1,380.00.

Morris Chair, 43" x 29½" x 35", FR, "Handcraft" decal, signed, $1,092.00.

Pedestals & Stands

Not Shown

27 Pedestal, square top, long corbels, 12" x 36", VG, $1,900.00.

28 Pedestal, original finish, 13" x 13" x 42", EX, $1,800.00.

Pedestal, long corbels, 14" x 48", VG, $5,000.00.

26 Smoker's Cabinet, rectangular top, single drawer, 20" x 15" x 29", VG, "Handcraft" decal, $3,500.00.

Smoker's Cabinet, 1904, single drawer, 20" x 16" x 30", EX, red decal, signed, $11,000.00.

24 Stand (plant), 14" x 14" x 28", VG, $475.00.

512 Stand, round, original finish, 28" x 24", VG, $1,500.00.

550 Stand, original finish, 29" x 20" x 18", VG, conjoined symbols, signature, $1,380.00.

573 Stand, round, original finish on base, 29" x 18", AVG+, "Handcraft" decal, signed, $1,200.00.

574 Stand, clipped corners, refinished, 29" x 18", AVG+, branded signature, $800.00.

Stand (plant), original finish, 24" x 12" x 12", VG, "work of" decal, signed, $1,610.00.

Stand, single drawer, refinished, 29" x 24" x 16", AVG+, "Handcraft" decal, signed, $1,100.00.

Stand (plant), refinished, 17¾" x 16" x 16", G, "Handcraft" decal, $275.00 – 300.00.

Stand (chafing), low shelf, 28" x 18" x 12", VG, $2,700.00.

Rockers

L. & J. G. Stickley spindled sewing rocker, with replaced brown leather seat and original finish. Good condition, 36" x 24" x 17½". $475.00.

L. & J. G. Stickley bow-arm rocker (model 427), with original finish with light overcoat, replaced leather, and "work of" decal. Signed, excellent condition, 38" x 31" x 30. $5,750.00. *Photo courtesy of Craftsman Auctions.*

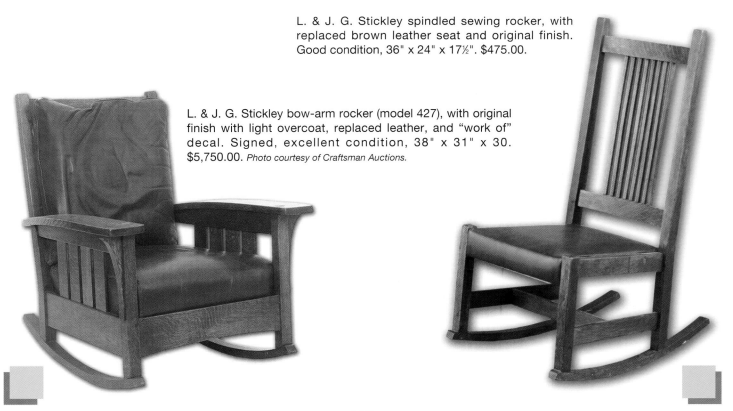

L. & J. G. Stickley sewing rocker, with center backslat flanked by two turned spindles, arched crest-rail, and turned front posts. Missing seat cushion, fair condition, 33½" x 18" x 23". $200.00 – 300.00.

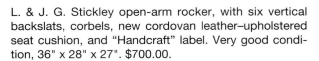

L. & J. G. Stickley open-arm rocker, with six vertical backslats, corbels, new cordovan leather–upholstered seat cushion, and "Handcraft" label. Very good condition, 36" x 28" x 27". $700.00.

L. & J. G. Stickley spindle-back mahogany sewing rocker, with inset new leather-covered seat and original finish. Good condition, 36" x 17" x 21". $275.00 – 350.00.

L. & J. G. Stickley open-arm rocker, with six vertical back-slats, drop-in seat cushion, and original finish with overcoat. "The work of" label, good condition, 40" x 28" x 28". $1,400.00.

L. & J. G. Stickley open-arm rocker, with six vertical back-slats, new dark brown leather-upholstered seat cushion, and worn original finish. Good condition, "the work of" decal, 38" x 27¾" x 31½". $1,300.00.

L. & J. G. Stickley open-arm rocker, with six vertical backslats, brown vinyl-upholstered seat cushion, original finish, and "Handcraft" decal. Good condition, 33" x 27" x 27". $600.00.

Not Shown

333 Rocker (sewing), 2 vertical slats to back, leather seat, 18" x 17" x 31", EX, "Handcraft" decal, $475.00.

401 Rocker, bent arms, 5 vertical slats, long corbels, EX, "work of" decal, signed, $2,550.00.

405 Rocker, 4 horizontal slats to back, open under arms, 25" x 31" x 34", VG, $280.00 – 300.00.

413 Rocker, arms, 37" x 34" x 37", VG, $2,500.00.

421 Rocker, open arms, corbels, arched rails, 31" x 29" x 39", EX, "work of" decal, signed, $1,600.00.

421 Rocker, arched seat rail, leather cushions, 31" x 33" x 38", VG, $850.00.

425 Rocker (sewing), 5 slats to back, leather cushion, 19" x 18" x 35", VG, "work of" decal, signed, $180.00 – 200.00.

427 Rocker, 4 vertical slats under arms, 31" x 32" x 39", VG, "Handcraft" decal, $2,900.00.

437 Rocker, refinished, 36" x 28" x 23", G, "Handcraft" decal, signed, $1,150.00.

437 Rocker, refinished, 37" x 28" x 25", G, $920.00.

451 Rocker, 6 slats to back, flat arms, corbels, 39" x 28" x 32", G, $1,400.00.

461 Rocker, 7 slats under each arm, 31" x 30" x 36", VG, "Handcraft" decal, $1,600.00.

475 Rocker, 6 slats to each side, corbels front and back, 25" x 23" x 40", VG, "work of" decal, signed, $3,250.00.

475 Rocker, deep, 6 slats under each arm, 32" x 35" x 36", VG, "work of" decal, signed, $2,700.00 – 3,250.00.

485 Rocker, 6 slats under each arm, 32" x 29" x 38", VG, $1,700.00.

487 Rocker, 6 slats to back, open under arms, drop-in seat, 28" x 25" x 39", EX, "Handcraft" decal, $1,200.00.

499 Rocker, slant arms, 5 slats under arms, 33" x 27" x 40", G, "Handcraft" decal, $1,500.00.

781½ Rocker, flat, 5 slats under arms, leather seat, 38" h, EX, $3,000.00.

809 Rocker, 5 vertical slats under top rail, drop-in spring cushion, 18" x 17" x 34", FR, $225.00 – 250.00.

817 Rocker, 5 vertical slats, open under arms, arched seat rail, 25" x 20" x 35", G, $350.00 – 400.00.

817 Rocker, 6 vertical slats to back, open under arms, 27" x 29" x 36", EX, "work of" decal, signed, $1,400.00.

819 Rocker, arms, 3 slats to back, leather seat, G, $700.00.

827 Rocker, 3 horizontal slats to back, leather cushion, 27" x 32" x 32", EX, "work of" decal, signed, $650.00 – 750.00.

859 Rocker, 6 slats, square tiles, drop-in seat, 25" x 20" x 35", G, $550.00.

Not Shown

Rocker, 5 vertical slats, open under arms, arched seat rail, spring cushion, 25" x 20" x 35", G, $350.00 – 400.00.

Rocker, 5 slats under each arm, arched seat rail, 30" x 36" x 38", EX, $1,400.00.

Rocker, 7 slats under each arm, 31" x 30" x 36", VG, "Handcraft" decal, $1,600.00.

Rocker, open arms, 32½" x 27" x 21", G, "Handcraft," signed, $632.00.

Rocker (sewing), 4 center backslats, 2 spindles, 33½" x 18" x 23", FR, $250.00 – 300.00.

Rocker, open arms, 6 vertical slats to back, 35" x 27" x 28¾", FR, $1,200.00.

Rocker, 6 vertical slats, 36" x 28" x 26", VG, "work of" decal, $700.00.

Rocker, original finish, 36" x 28" x 23", FR, $575.00.

Rocker, original finish, replaced leather seat, 37" x 28" x 25", G, signed, $1,380.00.

Servers

L. & J. G. Stickley server, with backsplash, three short drawers over one long drawer, one shelf, hammered-copper pulls, and fair original finish. "The work of" brand, very good condition, 45" x 44¼" x 18¼". $2,500.00.

L. & J. G. Stickley server, with backsplash, overhanging top, arched apron, and two lower shelves. Refinished, very good condition, 38½" x 40" x 15". $2,700.00.

Settles

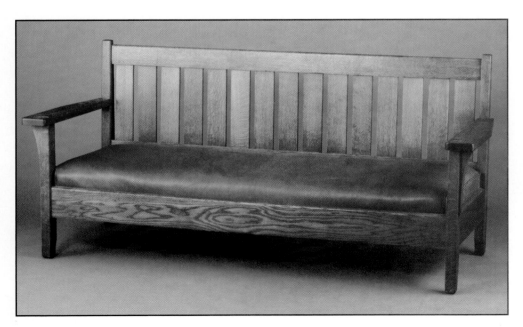

L. & J. G. Stickley drop-arm settle, with vertical backslats, drop-in spring seat, new brown leather upholstery, good new finish, and "Handcraft" mark. Good condition, 36" x 77" x 29". $1,800.00.

L. & J. G. Stickley rare crib settle (model 222), with vertical slats to back and sides, tapering posts, beveled rail, and new dark brown leather drop-in seat. Original finish, "the work of" label, excellent condition, 76" x 36" x 31". $11,000.00.

L. & J. G. Stickley even-arm settle, with five wide vertical backslats, square posts, and one wide vertical slat to each side. Missing drop-in seat cushion, some restoration to mostly original finish, "the work of" decal, signed. Excellent condition, 28" x 72" x 27". $2,400.00 – 3,000.00.

L. & J. G. Stickley cube settle, with broad horizintal panels to the back and under each arm, brown leather cushions, very good original-condition upholsterery on spring seat, and "the work of" decal. Excellent condition, 28" x 72" x 27". $2,400.00 – 3,000.00.

L. & J. G. Stickley open-arm settle, with cloud-lift crestrail, horizontal backslats, corbels under open arms, new tan leather-upholstered seat cushion, and "the work of" label. Very good condition, 36" x 53" x 26". $1,100.00.

L. & J. G. Stickley parlor set consisting of settle, armchair, and rocker, each with corbels under open arms, back and seat reupholstered in tacked-on brown vinyl, worn finish, and loose joinery. The settle is unmarked. Fair condition, 36¼" x 52½" x 22½". $1,500.00 – 2,000.00.

L. & J. G. Stickley tall-back settle, with open arms, vertical backslats, slats to the floor from the seat rails, and drop-in seat cushion. Refinished, reupholstered, "the work of" label, good condition, 45" x 58" x 23". $3,500.00.

L. & J. G. Stickley drop-arm settle (model 261), with enhanced finish and replaced leather. Very good condition, 38" x 64" x 26". $2,012.00. *Photo courtesy of Craftsman Auctions.*

L. & J. G. Stickley drop-arm settle, with replaced leather. Average condition, refinished, 37" x 72" x 22½". $1,600.00 – 2,200.00.
Photo courtesy of Craftsman Auctions.

L. & J. G. Stickley drop-arm settle (model 225), in original finish with light overcoat, with replaced leather. Signed, "work of" decal, very good condition, 37" x 53" x 22½". $2,242.00.
Photo courtesy of Craftsman Auctions.

Not Shown

Hall Seat, 2 horizontal boards to back, 60" x 20" x 38", EX, "Handcraft," signed, $5,500.00.

206 Settle, 13 vertical slats to back, wood seat, 68" x 22" x 37", G, $800.00.

215 Settle, even arms, 2 slats under arms, 7 slats to back, 72" x 26" x 36", EX, "Handcraft" decal, $2,100.00.

221 Settle, tall tapered posts, 16 slats to back, 7 slats to each side, 60" x 30" x 39", EX, red decal, $7,500.00.

222 Settle, even arms, 7 slats under arms, 20 slats to back, 76" x 36" x 39", EX, "work of decal", signed, $13,000.00.

223 Settle, tall tapered posts, 22 slats to back, 7 slats to sides, 84" x 32" x 39", EX, "Handcraft" decal, $11,000.00.

225 Settle and 882 Armchair, original finish, 36" x 37" x 21", FR, chair has "Handcraft" decal, $1,250.00.

225 Settle, 13 slats to back, drop-in spring cushion, 53" x 23" x 37", VG, "Handcraft" decal, $1,700.00.

229 Settle, wide horizontal board to back, 2 vertical slats, 71" x 26" x 35", VG, $3,000.00.

232 Settle, 1 wide slat to sides, 5 wide slats to back, 72" x 27" x 28", EX, branded signature, $4,250.00.

263 Settle, 2 slats under arm, 7 slats to back, 77" x 29" x 37", EX, "work of" decal, signed, $5,500.00.

275 Settle, even arms, spring cushion, pegged rails, 84" x 32" x 40", VG, "Handcraft," signed, $8,000.00.

280 Settle, even arms, beveled posts, 12 slats to back, 60" x 31" x 34", VG, "work of" decal, signed, $4,750.00.

281 Settle, capped arms & back, spring cushion, 77" x 31" x 34", EX, "Handcraft" decal, $7,000.00.

285 Settle, even arms, 2 slats under each arm, 7 wide slats to back, 70" x 27" x 34", EX, "work of" decal, signed, $5,500.00.

Settle, posts through flat open arms, 36¾" x 63" x 22¾", VG, "work of" decal, signed, $2,500.00.

Settle, original leather back & seat, 41½" x 40½", EX, "Onondaga Shops" paper label, $1,200.00.

Settle, drop arms, 12 slats back, drop-in cushion, 65" x 36" x 25", VG, $2,800.00.

Settle, 13 vertical slats to back, wooden seat, 68" x 22" x 37", G, $800.00.

Settle, even arms over 4 slats, 15 slats to back, 72" x 26" x 39", EX, "Onondaga Shops," $9,500.00.

Sideboards

L. & J. G. Stickley sideboard, with plate rail, two doors with hammered-copper strap hinges and pulls, and four drawers over a linen drawer. Refinished, "Handcraft" decal, excellent condition, 48¼" x 54" x 24". $5,500.00.

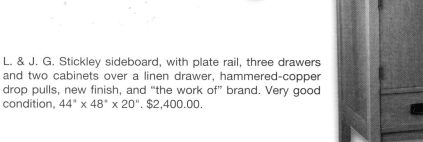

L. & J. G. Stickley sideboard, with plate rail, three drawers and two cabinets over a linen drawer, hammered-copper drop pulls, new finish, and "the work of" brand. Very good condition, 44" x 48" x 20". $2,400.00.

L. & J. G. Stickley sideboard, with plate rail backsplash, four small drawers, hammered-copper strap hardware on two cabinet doors, linen drawer, replaced bottom middle drawer. Parts of backsplash have been replaced as well. Refinished, repatinated, fair condition, 46¾" x 56" x 22". $3,250.00.

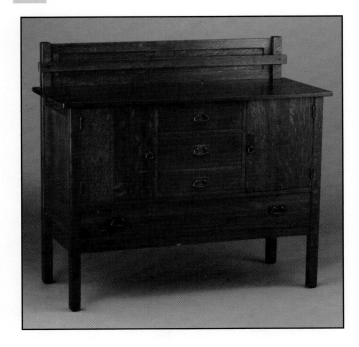

L. & J. G. Stickley sideboard, with plate rail, three center drawers flanked by cabinets, large linen drawer, hammered-copper pulls, good original finish, and branded mark. Very good condition, 44" x 48" x 20". $4,000.00.

L. & J. G. Stickley "Onondaga Shops" sideboard (model 737), with plate shelf over mirror backsplash, two paneled cabinet doors with strap hinges, four center drawers, linen drawer, and good original finish. Good condition, 62" x 51" x 24". $4,500.00 – 5,000.00.

L. & J. G. Stickley sideboard, with plate rail backsplash, four center drawers, two paneled cabinet doors with strap hardware and copper pulls, linen drawer, original finish, and "Handcraft" label. Very good condition, 48½" x 54" x 25". $5,500.00.

L. & J. G. Stickley sideboard (model 737), with strap hinges. Good condition, refinished, 62" x 54" x 24". 4,500.00 – $5,000.00. *Photo courtesy of Craftsman Auctions.*

L. & J. G. Stickley sideboard (model 735). Refinished, good condition, 46½" x 56" x 22. $1,840.00. *Photo courtesy of Craftsman Auctions.*

L. & J. G. Stickley sideboard (model 731) with strap hinges and original finish with overcoating. Above average condition, signed, 49½" x 72" x 25". $6,500.00. *Photo courtesy of Craftsman Auctions.*

L. & J. G. Stickley sideboard (model 745), with strap hinges. Excellent condition, refinished, signed, "Handcraft," 48" x 54" x 24". $5,000.00 – 7,000.00.

Not Shown

740 Server, 2 drawers, 2 shelves, copper hardware, 48" x 11" x 50", G, "Handcraft" decal, signed, $1,000.00.

741 Server, copper pulls, refinished, 40" x 44" x 18", EX, decal, $3,000.00.

741 Server, copper pulls, original finish, 44" x 18" x 39", EX, $2,500.00.

752 Server, refinished top, 39" x 40", VG, "Handcraft" decal, $1,500.00.

709 Sideboard, paneled plate rail, curved shelf, 54" x 22" x 48", EX, "work of" decal, $3,500.00.

731 Sideboard, side cabinets, 4 drawers, linen drawer, copper hardware, 72" x 26" x 50", VG, $3,000.00.

734 Sideboard, 3 drawers, 2 cabinets, 1 long drawer, 48" x 20" x 44", VG, "Handcraft" decal, $2,800.00.

735 Sideboard, 4 short drawers, 1 long drawer, 2 cabinet doors, 56" x 23" x 45", VG, $2,400.00.

738 Sideboard, 5 drawers, 2 cabinet doors, copper hinges, 60" x 21" x 46", EX, $4,500.00.

745 Sideboard, narrow drawers, 1 long drawer, 2 cabinet doors, 54" x 24" x 48", EX, "Handcraft" decal, $6,500.00.

Sideboard, 4 drawers, linen drawer, 38¼" x 54" x 24¼", AI, $1,400.00.

Sideboard, 6 drawers, refinished, 48¼" x 54" x 24", EX, "Handcraft" decal, $5,500.00.

Sideboard, 4 center drawers, 1 long drawer, 54" x 24" x 42", FR, "work of" decal, signed, $3,250.00.

Sideboard, mirrored backsplash, shelf, 4 drawers, 62¼" x 53¼", EX, $4,000.00.

Set of six L. & J. G. Stickley dining side chairs, each with curved crestrail over three vertical backslats, reupholstered brown leather, and original finish. Excellent condition, 37" x 17¾" x 16¾". $7,500.00.

Set of six L. & J. G. Stickley side chairs, each with arched crestrail, five vertical backslats, drop-in seat cushion recovered in tan leather, and branded mark. Refinished, excellent condition, 38½" x 17" x 17". $3,500.00.

Two L. & J. G. Stickley spindle-back side chairs (model 330), each with original brown leather-covered seat, original finish, and "Handcraft" decal. Very good condition, 36½" x 16" x 15". $1,700.00.

L. & J. G. Stickley mahogany spindle-back side chair, with reupholstered seat and original finish. Good condition, 41¼" x 17½" x 16¼". $375.00 – 400.00.

Not Shown

323 Side chair, 6 vertical slats, arched top rail, 19" x 18" x 37½", EX, branded signature, $650.00.

332 Side chair, plank seat, G, paper label, $230.00.

368 Side chairs (pair), 3 vertical slats to back, 17" x 15" x 34", EX, red decal, $600.00.

800 Side chair, original finish, 36" x 18" x 17", G, "work of" decal, signed, $488.00.

1313 Side chair, 3 vertical backslats, leather seat, 36" x 16" x 16", G, $275.00 – 300.00.

1340 Side chairs (set of 4), 3 vertical slats to back, refinished, 18" x 17" x 35", VG, $1,100.00.

Side chair, 8 spindles to back, 17.5" x 16" x 39.5", EX, handcraft decal, $1,100.00.

Side chair, 5 vertical slats, seat rails, 35¾" x 19½" x 18½", G, "Handcraft" decal, $175.00 – 200.00.

Side chairs (pair), 5 vertical backslats, refinished, 36" x 19¾" x 17¾", G, "work of" decal, signed, $900.00.

Side chair, spindled, 36½" x 16" x 15", G, "Handcraft" decal, signed, $650.00 – 750.00.

Side chair, inverted U crestrail, 5 backslats, 37" x 19¾" x 20", G, "Onondaga Shops," $325.00 – 350.00.

Side chair, inverted U crestrail, 5 backslats, 39" x 18" x 18", G, "Handcraft" decal, $475.00 - 500.00.

L. & J. G. Stickley mousehole trestle table, with overhanging rectangular top, broad stretcher keyed through cut-out plank sides, and cleaned original finish. Very good condition, "the work of" decal, 29¼" x 48" x 32". $3,000.00.

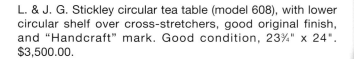

L. & J. G. Stickley circular tea table (model 608), with lower circular shelf over cross-stretchers, good original finish, and "Handcraft" mark. Good condition, 23¾" x 24". $3,500.00.

L. & J. G. Stickley encylopedia table, with square overhanging top, two divided shelves with vertical slats, and original finish. Excellent condition, 29¼" x 27" x 27". $10,000.00.

L. & J. G. Stickley lamp table, with clip-corner top, cross-stretchers mortised through the legs, and good original finish. Good condition, 29" x 36" x 36". $1,500.00 – 2,000.00.

L. & J. G Stickley rare trestle table, with lower shelf mortised through trestle sides. Refinished, "the work of" decal, very good condition, 29" x 60" x 36". $2,500.00 – 3,500.00.

L. & J. G. Stickley mousehole trestle table, with up-ended stretcher keyed through the sides, good original finish, and branded mark. Very good condition, 29" x 48" x 32". $2,400.00.

L. & J. G. Stickley tea table (model 539), circa 1910, with over-hanging circular top and arched stretchers with through-tenons. Good condition, 29" x 42". $1,600.00 – 2,000.00.

L. & J. G. Stickley circular lamp table, with apron and lower shelf supported by arched cross-stretchers mortised through the legs. Refinished, very good condition, 29" x 36". $1,300.00.

L. & J. G. Stickley trestle table, with lower shelf mortised through trestle sides. Refinished, "the work of" decal, very good condition, 29" x 60" x 36". $4,000.00 – 5,000.00.

L. & J. G. Stickley rare mousehole trestle library table, with rectangular top and sideways stretcher mortised and keyed through the legs, original finish to base, and new finish to top. Excellent condition, 29" x 60" x 32". $3,250.00.

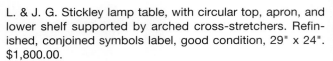

L. & J. G. Stickley lamp table, with circular top, apron, and lower shelf supported by arched cross-stretchers. Refinished, conjoined symbols label, good condition, 29" x 24". $1,800.00.

L. & J. G. Stickley lamp table, with circular top and apron, cross-stretchers mortised through the legs, and "Handcraft" decal. Very good condition, 29" x 36". $950.00 – 1,400.00.

L. & J. G. Stickley mousehole trestle table (model 599), with rectangular top, keyed broad stretcher, good original finish to base, and original finish to top. Excellent condition, 29" x 48" x 32". $2,000.00.

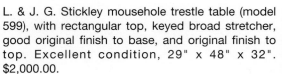

Not Shown

22 Table, copper-sheathed top, X-stretcher, 28" x 17¾", EX, $3,750.00.

381 Table, circular top, through-post construction, 36" x 30", VG, $900.00 – 1,000.00.

508 Table, 2 tiers, circular top, 24" x 24", VG, $2,600.00.

516 Table (book), 7 slats, bookshelf on all sides, 27" x 29", VG , "Handcraft" decal, $9,000.00.

536 Table, round top, curved apron, through-tenon construction, 24" x 29", VG, "Handcraft" decal, $1,100.00.

536 Table, round top over curved apron, through-tenon construction, 36" x 29", VG, "work of" decal, signed, $950.00 – 1,000.00.

538 Table, circular top, with apron, arched cross-stretchers, 30" x 29", VG, branded signature, $1,100.00.

541 Table (lamp), circular top, apron, lower shelf, 30" x 29", EX, "Handcraft," signed, $5,500.00.

543 Table, circular top, lower shelf, 36" x 29", VG, branded signature, $1,200.00.

543 Table, circular top, over lower shelf, 42" x 29", VG, $1,300.00.

558 Table, octagonal top, exposed leg joints, 17" w, VG, $400.00.

558 Table, octagonal top, X-stretchers, 20" x 18", G, $1,100.00.

572 Table (game), square top w/cut corners, 30" x 30" x 26", G, branded signature, $950.00 – 1,300.00.

573 Table (lamp), circular top over lower shelf, 24" x 29", VG, "work of" decal, signed, $1,400.00.

574 Table (side), 18" x 29", VG, "work of" decal, $800.00.

575 Table (lamp), 23" x 24", G, $285.00 – 300.00.

575 Table, round shelf, arched stretchers, 24" x 29", EX, $1,000.00 – 1,100.00.

576 Table (side), cut corners, lower square shelf, 24" x 29", VG, $650.00.

577 Table, circular top, round shelf, 36" x 30", VG, red decal, $700.00.

579 Table (lamp), 29" x 35½", G, $862.50

589 Table, tilt-top mechanism, 20" x 24", VG, "work of" decal, signed, $1,500.00.

590 Table, drop leaf, 24" x 24", EX, "work of" decal, signed, $3,250.00.

594 Table (trestle), large top, 72" x 45" x 29", EX, "work of" decal, signed, $8,500.00.

598 Table, 54" x 32" x 29", VG, $2,100.00.

599 Table (trestle), mousehole, 29" x 54" x 32", EX, $2,500.00.

599 Table, slab sides, vertical stretcher, 48" x 32" x 29", EX, "work of" decal, signed, $5,000.00.

Not Shown

599 Table (trestle), mousehole, rectangular top, 29" x 48" x 32", VG, $2,400.00.

Tables (tea, pair), arched stretchers, 20" x 26", EX, "L. & J." brand, $2,000.00.

Table (half), 22" x 13" x 30", G, $450.00.

Table (tea), rectangular top, 26" x 17" x 24", EX, "Handcraft" decal, signed, $11,000.00.

Table (lamp), 28" x 30", G, $800.00.

Table (lamp), round, 28½" x 35½", G, $1,610.00.

Table, round top, round shelf, 36" x 30", EX, $2,500.00.

Table, rectangular top, 4 splayed legs, 48" x 15" x 16", VG, "work of" decal, signed, $4,000.00.

Table, rectangular top, mousehole, 48" x 33" x 29", VG, conjoined symbols decal, $1,600.00.

Table (lamp), circular top, refinished, 29½" x 36", VG, "work of" decal, signed, $1,800.00.

Table (lamp), mahogany base, 23" x 14", G, "Handcraft" decal, $800.00.

Table (lamp), circular overhanging top, 29½" x 30", G, $700.00.

Table (lamp), 29" x 29½" x 29½", VG, "Onondaga Shops," $1,495.00.

Not Shown

554 Tabouret, square top, open legs, 15" x 18", EX, branded signature, $1,000.00.

558 Tabouret, octagonal, original finish, 17" x 15", VG, "work of" decal, signed, $1,300.00.

559 Tabouret, refinished, 18" x 20", VG, "work of" decal, signed, $1,000.00.

560 Tabouret, 18" x 16", VG, "work of" decal, signed, $500.00 – 600.00.

562 Tabouret, 20" x 22", VG, $1,600.00.

Tabouret, cut-corner top, arched stretcher, 16" x 16" x 18", EX, "Handcraft" decal, signed, $800.00.

L. & J. G. Stickley clip-corner tabouret, with legs mortised through the octagonal top, arched stretchers, new finish, and decal. Very good condition, 17" x 15". $1,300.00.

L. & J. G. Stickley octagonal tabouret, with posts through the top and arched cross-stretchers. Refinished, "the work of" decal, good condition, 20" x 18". $950.00.

Charles Stickley Furniture
(Early 1900s)

When the Stickley Brothers Furniture Company was founded in 1901, the firm was located in Binghampton, New York. Another factory was later opened in Grand Rapids, Michigan. Albert and John Stickley ran the company in Michigan, and Charles ran the company in Binghampton. He and an uncle operated the business for several years as the Stickley/Brandt Furniture Company. Much of the furniture produced by Charles Stickley during this period is found signed "Charles Stickley" or with a Stickley/Brandt decal, and is usually found without a model number. This furniture brings high prices, but does not bring as much as other Stickley furniture, even though pieces signed by Charles Stickley rarely ever show up at auction. Still, it is most sought after at Stickley auctions around the country by some collectors.

While writing this guide, I found that very few pieces of Charles Stickley furniture have shown up on the auction blocks of catalog auctions in the last five years. In that time, only three armchairs have shown up, and only one library table has shown up. I have come to believe that either Charles Stickley produced very little furniture on his own, or that it has become very scarce over the years. I have also come to believe that Charles specialized more in making rockers and settles than he did any other furniture. If you have furniture that was made by Charles Stickley, or that has the Stickley/Brandt decal, please write to me at PO Box 808, Belpre Ohio 45714.

Armchairs

Not Shown

Armchairs (pair), corbels, slats under arms, 28" x 24" x 37", EX, $700.00 pair.

Armchair, heavily constructed, cutouts, 29" x 23" x 36", VG, $1,700.00.

Armchair, U-back over 3 slats, drop-in spring cushion, 29" x 24" x 35", VG, $750.00.

Chair, 9 spindles to back, drop-in cushions, 18" x 17" x 36", EX, branded, $450.00.

Charles Stickley armchair, with cut-out back panels, vertical slats, new tan leather-covered drop-in spring seat, overcoat on original finish, and decal on back. Good condition, 36½" x 29½" x 23". $1,100.00.

Bookcases

Not Shown

Bookcase, single door, 16 panes, copper, 36" x 13" x 56", VG, $3,250.00.

Bookcase, single door, 16 panes, brass hardware, EX, $3,500.00.

Bookcase, open, slab sides, chamfered back, 41½" x 11" x 56", VG, $3,000.00.

Chests of Drawers

Not Shown

Chest of Drawers, 2 drawers over 4, wooden pulls, 38" x 20" x 55", EX, $2,300.00.

Chest of Drawers, 2 half drawers over 4 full, 40" x 22" x 53", VG, $4,250.00.

Library Tables

Charles Stickley library table, with two drawers. Signed, overcoated, good condition, 30" x 48" x 30". $1,092.00. *Photo courtesy of Craftsman Auctions.*

Morris Chairs

Not Shown

Morris Chair, 31" x 35" x 39", G, impressed signature, $700.00.

Morris Chair, 4 slats under arms, 32" x 34" x 39", VG, signed, $700.00.

Chair, 9 spindles to back, drop-in cushion, 18" x 17" x 36", EX, $450.00.

Rockers

Set of two Charles Stickley rockers, one with four vertical backslats and one with upholstered back. Both have maroon velvet seat cushions and original finish. Both marked, good condition, 42" x 29½" x 28". $500.00.

Charles Stickley rocker, with open arms, cut-out back panels, vertical slats, new tan leather-covered drop-in spring seat, overcoat to original finish, and decal. Good condition, 34" x 30" x 28". $1,300.00.

Charles Stickley rocker, with open arms, cut-out back panel, crestrail, and fabric-upholstered seat cushion. Good condition, 33¼" x 30" x 30". $900.00 – 1,000.00.

Not Shown

Rocker, armless, 3 slats to back, leather seat, 19" x 19" x 34", VG, $140.00 – 150.00.

Rocker, drop-in cushion, 23" x 29" x 37", VG, $1,000.00.

Rocker, 3 horizontal slats, 28" x 24" x 35", VG, $290.00.

Rockers (pair), corbels and slats under arms, 30" x 29" x 34", VG, $850.00.

Rocker, slats, 36" x 29" x 27", G, branded mark, Quaint decal, $475.00.

Rocker, slats, originial finish, 37½" x 29" x 28", G, branded mark, signed, $500.00.

Servers

Not Shown

Charles Stickley double-drawer server, with backsplash, over-hanging rectangular top, brass pulls, and original finish. Signed "Charles Stickley," good condition, 35" x 42½" x 20". $1,500.00.

Charles Stickley open-arm settle, with cut-out back panels, mortised front stretcher and crest-rail, new tan leather-covered drop-in spring seat, overcoat to original finish, and Stickley/Brandt label. Fair condition, 36½" x 60" x 26½". $2,100.00.

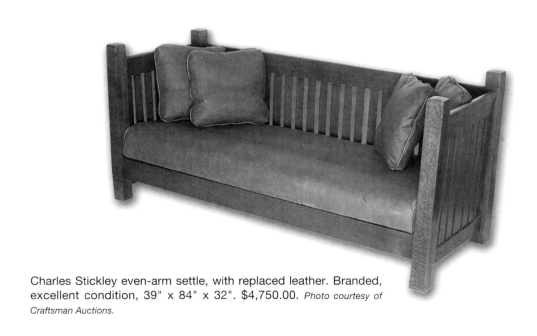

Charles Stickley even-arm settle, with replaced leather. Branded, excellent condition, 39" x 84" x 32". $4,750.00. *Photo courtesy of Craftsman Auctions.*

Not Shown

Settle, drop arms, 59" x 27" x 37", VG, decal, $2,800.00.

Settle, drop arms, through-tenons, 5 slats under arms, 14 slats to back, 76" x 33" x 35", EX, $3,000.00.

Sideboards

Not Shown

Sideboard, paneled plate rail, 4 drawers, 43" x 56" x 22½", VG, $2,500.00.

Sideboard, paneled plate rail, corbeled shelf, 56" x 22" x 53", VG, $3,500.00.

Sideboard, 2 small drawers over 2 large, oval pulls, 70" x 25" x 51", VG, $2,600.00.

Tables

Not Shown

Table (lamp), circular top, lower shelf, 29" x 30", VG, Stickley & Brandt, $2,000.00.

Table (side), single drawer, ring pulls, 30" x 19½" x 30" , VG, $5,500.00.

Charles Stickley lamp table, with circular top, lower shelf over cross-stretchers mortised through the legs, very good original finish, and Stickley/Brandt decal. Very good condition, 29" x 30". $2,000.00.

Charles Stickley parlor set consisting of settle, rocker, and armchair. Settle is in original finish; rocker and armchair have some color loss and overcoating. There is a repair to rocker arm. Rocker & settle are signed. Armchair is 37" x 30" x 22½", rocker is 34" x 30" x 22½", settle is 37" x 59" x 27". Fair condition. $5,175.00. *Photo courtesy of Craftsman Auctions.*

Reproduction Stickley Furniture

Today, the L. & J. G. Stickley Furniture Company of Manlius, New York, has been making exact replicas of original Stickley Arts and Crafts furniture. The new Stickley spindle chair they recently made is virtually identical to the original Gustav Stickley spindle chair that was first shown in 1905 Stickley catalog. This spindle chair has confused many; more than one person has believed he or she had a very valuable chair, only to find out that it was a reproduction. The new chairs are hand-made of quartersawn white oak and constructed with complex joints. They have keyed tenons and dovetails, just as the originals do. Today, an original Gustav Stickley spindle armchair can sell for as much as $3,000 to 4,000; a 1990s Stickley spindle chair of the same design can sell for $900.00.

Here is a list of Stickley marks and the dates they were used. Original tags on furniture were usually marked as being made in Syracuse or Fayetteville, New York; any tag today found on furniture that reads "Manlius, New York," is actually indicative of a reproduction.

Stickley Furniture Marks

Gustav Stickley
1901 – 1916

The Onondaga Shops
L. & J. G Stickley
1905

L & J. G. Stickley
1906 – 1912

L & J. G. Stickley
1912 – 1917

Stickley Associated Cabinetmakers
1916 – 1919

Stickley Brothers
Stickley Fayetteville Syracuse
1926 – 1977

Stickley Brothers
Fayetteville, NY
1927 – 1935

Leapold Stickley
1950 – Present

Stickley Brothers
1985 – Present

Gustav Stickley
Craftsman Workshops
1989 – Present

L. &J. G. Stickley Furniture
Company
New Tag and Burned Mark
Reproduction
Present mark

Stickley Brothers Furniture Company
1898 – 1916

Stickley Brothers Furniture Company
Grand Rapids, Michigan
1898 – 1916

Stickley & Brandt Chair Company
Binghampton, NY
1891 – 1919

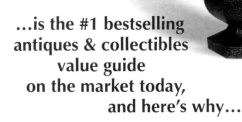